AF539211

CHILD ABUSE

By

Dr. Alaka Mishra

Senior Lecturer
Ganjam Law College
Bhanjavihar, Berhampur - 10
Ganjam Odisha
(INDIA)

DISCOVERY PUBLISHING HOUSE PVT. LTD.
NEW DELHI-110 002

Published by:
Tilak Wasan
DISCOVERY PUBLISHING HOUSE PVT. LTD.
4383/4B, Ansari Road, Darya Ganj
New Delhi-110 002 (India)
Phone : +91-11-23279245, 43596064-65
Fax : +91-11-23253475
E-mail : discoverypublishinghouse@gmail.com
sales@discoverypublishinggroup.com
parul.wasan@gmail.com
web : www.discoverypublishinggroup.com

***First Edition:* 2014**

ISBN: 978-93-5056-511-7

Child Abuse

Printed at:
Dynamic Printers
Delhi

ESTD. 1983

Tel. No. 0680-2290859

OFFICE OF THE

GANJAM LAW COLLEGE

BERHAMPUR - 760010, GANJAM.

No. .... Date 21/09/2013

Prof. (Dr.) N. S. J. Rao
B.Sc. (H), M.A.LL.M.,
Ph.D. (Law), D. Litt. (Law)
Principal Ganjam Law College,
Berhampur - 10, Odisha
Tel. No. 0680-2404259,
Cell: 09437385333

Res.: Braja Nagar,
2nd Line Extention,
Behind TV Station,
Berhampur - 760001, Orissa.
Ph. No. - 0680 - 2220309,
Cell: 09437885333

Foreword

At the dawn of this modern century mankind is experienced with rapid challenges and more experiences the traditional can advance to see the new horizon of development. In reality "Necessity creates the law; it supersedes rules; and whatever it reasonable in such cases is likewise legal".

Child is the gift of god; Children are represented as the most precious wealth and productive feature citizen of a country. They are considered as a 'poll of human potential' on which the dignity of nation depends upon thus the position and significance of children in a country across with all cultures and regions remain undebated but child abuse has been a matter of debate for long, now and across the world.

In the era of digital economy child became a commercial product for exploit and abuse is very widely spreads and popular phenomenon with shucking characteristic. Sexual violence against children occurs across all strata of society and in all countries of the world. Violence or any form of abuse against children in our society what is to be treated as heinous offence against mankind. It is usually silent, invisible and hidden crime that both boys and girls face at inside and outside at all corner of the society. The facts pertaining to juvenile delinquency falls with in two categories *i.e.*, Subjective approaches, and objective approaches and also the reformative, rehabilitate approaches are in boon.

Children are people with dignity; they have to be respected as those of adults. Indeed the children conditions are extremely gloomy and pathetic due to social and economic conditions, despite ongoing changes with in their ecological context.

Research says that more children are abused in every form in every respect. It became export commodity to sex tourism, trafficking, cyber crimes, pornography, terrorism, organ transplantation, and other modern organized crime merge with traditional crime like kidnapping, rape, prostitution, assault, murder, mutiny are some problems with peculiar and enormous in nature. Child marriage is against the law and also a social evil, which is gross violation of all categories of child rights. It is expressed that rising problems and many more challenges in the legal arena to find out the problems and suitable solution for it.

This book '*Child Abuse*' wrote in a simple language and lucid deception. The core presentation has also highlighted the methods and techniques and innovative approach, which explores many hidden facts on child abuse, neglect and exploitation in different parts of the country. I had a great pleasure in going through the book. In view of the dearth of books in this subject, this book will be useful to teachers, researchers, students, policy-makers, social activists and general readers, who are concerned with the subject and who desire to have knowledge of the subject.

PRINCIPAL.

PRINCIPAL,
Ganjam Law College
Berhampur (Gm.)

Preface

I would not probably have had the urge to write law books but the profound inspiration upcoming encouragement of my beloved father a senior advocate of Ganjam Bar Association and my teachers and well wisher always encourage me for intellectual contribution for development of law and its education and my college staff and students and my family members persuaded one to write books in socio legal issues that is useful to the students at a large.

My well wisher, Dr. Prakash Chandra Mishra, Prof. Commerce department of P. G. Studies at Bhanjavihar, Berhampur, Odisha, encouraged me to publish the same by a reputed publisher who have already published many books in India, who came forwarded to publish my literature in a short span of time and also taken well attention to publish this work with overwhelming response in every respect. The global problem of the present day is the socio legal issues and hence the captioned subject child abuse has attained greater importance and more research work is need of the hour.

From the very inception of civilization people have realized that proper child development was the key to their perpetuation. The significance and the importance of the child lie in the fact that the child is the universe. If there was no child, there would be no humanity and there cannot be universe without humanity. Mankind is a creation of God, "the indivisible and Almighty, child is considered to be most intellectual gene. Man in greed for socio-economic progress and in his curiosity to probe into and understand the philosophy of the creation of God, man has initiated the exploitation of not only his co-human and other beings, but also the beauty of natural resources. In this process man has reached an extreme stage of exploitation to his own generation and environment. Every child is the precious resource of the country. The strength of a nation is reflected within all-round development of the children, who are destined to be successful citizens of tomorrow. Children are the foundation of a nation and the future course of progress is determined by their physical and mental well-being which depend on their "right to survival, protection, development and participation is to protect and promote the well being of the children" in the society.

Child abuse is a phenomenon that has existed as long as families have existed. This research study provides much more information about the magnitude of child abuse and girl child neglect, in this report it is established that child abuse is rampant in India and the incidence is much higher than the general perceptions, while the situation is alarming. The forms of abuse are reflected in various reports about violence. But it is a crucial aspect to draw keen attention about what type of Violence and how many types of violence that exist in the society. These could be analysed in broader aspects, according to the context as three types of abuses which are generally occur in the society, *i.e.,* self-directed abuse, inter-personal abuse and collective abuse. The term 'Child Abuse' may have different connotations in different cultural milieu and socio-economic situations. Child abuse is very widespread and familiar phenomenon and a shocking characteristic of modern world. In today's scenario, it has become a very common incident when the innocent, defenseless, helpless child goes through physical, sexual and emotional abuse or even up to death. The effects of this trauma can be very deep and can last for life long period, which destroys the very roots of his or her physical and mental makeup. Thorough studies have shown that negligence and emotional abuse of child, which is so common every day, leaves much deeper impact on his/her mind than of physical abuse. Child at tourism is an item of the super market purchased by the customers as an article or treated as marketable commodity. For child prostitution,

Child Trafficking, Child sex tourism, child pornography and abuse of boy Child, the cyber space has became a fertile field for illegal activity and often lead to violent crimes. The possible cause is pornographic activity, stalker activity where there is likelihood of children being victim. The future of nation is sold on road side betel shop/cyber café; an absolute picture of crime as well as juvenile offender situation is un-predictable. If one from of abuse is prohibited it takes another nomenclature and exploitation at a gravity.

At the dawn of the 21st century human life is an experienced uncertainties and mounting stresses, which are un-denied and inevitable in every spheres of life. Tomorrow's world may be influenced by science and technology, but more than anything, it is already taking shape in the bodies and minds of our children. It explicitly specifies the duty of mankind in discharging their responsibility towards the promotion and protection of the rights of the children in their future well-being. Child is a bud, it nourishes in this conducive environment. It is not an exaggeration to say that the children are the blooming flowers of garden of society and so, it is our duty to protect these flowers from damaging effects of excessive exposure to heat, cold, and rain etc. Children are valuable asset and indeed they are the building blocks of nations and all of humanity. The concepts of Globalisation, Liberalization and Modernisation and Cyberism have given rise to many more challenges in the legal arena to find out the problems. But the problems like child exploitation, neglect, abuse, child trafficking, cyber crimes, pornography, sex tourism, terrorism and other modern organized crime problems are peculiar and enormous in nature. It is very difficult to sort out and solve them in accordance to law with in a stipulated period of time but this is not an impossible task. It is a fact that child abuse illuminates and influences the entire legal system of any civilized society. Laws cannot be enforced in the absence of a favorable consensus. A strong will to uplift the plight of the child coupled with strong legislative and legal measures will improve the situation.

–Author

Contents

1 Introduction

> *"To Look into some aspects of the future, we don't need projections by super computers much of the next millennium can be seen in how we care for our children today, Tomorrow's world may be influenced by science and technology but, more than anything. It is already taking shape in the bodies and minds of our children".*
>
> ***Koffi Annan***

In this juncture of 21st century, human life is an experience of uncertainties and mounting with stresses, which are un-denied and inevitable in every spheres of life. Man is born in a family and dies in a family in a given society. Family is one of the social institutions and plays a significant role in the care and development of children. Family nourishes, educates, protects and shapes the destiny of its members. Children were considered as a pool of human potentials, on which the destiny of a nation depends. Children are considered as the Gift of God. Yes, God has created human beings as equal without any discrimination as to their skill power, will power, grasping power, intellectual power, etc. Changes in family membership and changes in any individual or relationship within the family are bound to affect the dynamics of the whole family. The need to understand the unique relationship between each parent and their children is a matter of concern in today's complex world. There is a large child population in India and a large percentage of this population is vulnerable to abuse, exploitation and neglect. Every child has the right to life and free from violence. The primary responsibility of protecting children from abuse and neglect lies with the families or the primary caregivers. However, communities and civil society and all other person are also responsible for the care and protection of children. The overarching responsibility always lies within the State and it is the State that has to create a protective environment and provide a safety net for children, who fall into vulnerable and exploitative situations.

The society, like a family must provide for the basic needs of children, as a first priority for its own survival and development. It is not an exaggeration to say that the children are the blooming flowers of garden of society and so it is our duty to protect these flowers from damaging effects of excessive exposure to heat, cold, and rain etc. Children are valuable assets and indeed they are the building blocks of nations and of humanity. There is also widespread acceptance, in principle, that children are entitled to fulfilment of their social and economic rights as well as special protection. Childhood is entitled to special care and assistance and children should grow up in an atmosphere of happiness, love and understanding. It has played an important role in promoting children as a priority in the making of the public policy, not just in the developing world but also in the rich countries. It is essential in this work to define child in accordance to law.

Definition of the Child

A child was defined as a person not having completed 18 years of age. In accordance to Article-1 under child is defined by the U.N. Convention on the Rights of the child as 'every human being below the age of 18 years unless under the law applicable to the child, majority is attained earlier'. The Convention clearly specifies the upper age limit for childhood as 18 years, but, the upper limit on childhood is specified as an age of 'childhood' rather than 'majority', recognising that in most legal systems, a child can acquire full legal capacity with regard to various matters at different ages.

1. Thus, while the Convention defines a 'child' as every human being below the age of 18 years, it allows for minimum age to be set, under different circumstances, balancing the evolving capacities of the child with the State's obligation to provide special protection. Accordingly, Indian legislation has defined minimum ages under various laws related to the protection of child rights.
2. With respect to the rights of the child in the womb, the legislation in India is in harmony with the interpretation of the Convention, incorporated in the Indian Constitution as 'right to life'. Significantly, Section 20 of the Indian Succession Act gives the right to property to a child in the womb whose parent dies intestate and who is subsequently born alive – he/she will have the same right to inherit as if he or she had been born before the death of the parent.
3. As per CRC's definition, childhood can be perceived as setting a basic minimum standard in view of Article 41, which declares that 'nothing in the Convention or any of its provisions shall effect realisation of the rights of the child' under the law of a State Party. It is essential that there is some synchronization of the upper age limit for childhood. India has achieved this to a large extent, for instance, the minimum compulsory age of education is 14 years. The various laws relating to labour prohibit a person under the age of 14 years to work. Those Acts are Child Labour (prohibition and regulation) Act, 1986. Merchant Shipping Act, 1958. Motor Transport Workers Act, 1951. Apprentices Act, 1961. Bidi and Cigar workers (Conditions of Employment) Act, 1966. Plantation and Labour Act, 1951. Factories Act, 1948. Similarly the minimum age at which compulsory education ends synchronizes with the minimum age of employment. The age of capacity to contract a marriage is 18 years for a

girl and 21 years for a boy, for all communities. The Child Marriage Restraint Act, 1929, defines a child as a person who, if a male, has not completed 21 years of age, and if a female, has not completed 18 years of age. Under Section 5 of this Act whoever performs, conducts or directs any child marriage shall be punishable with simple imprisonment up to three months and shall also be liable to fine, unless he proves that he had reason to believe that the marriage was not a child marriage. But the new law for prohibition of sexual offence under consensual sex age has reduced to 2 years *i.e.* 16 years. However, regarding certain aspects that are deeply rooted in the community, and compounded by historical poverty and vulnerable socio-economic conditions, there is a gap between laws and their enforcement.

Every child is the precious resource of the country. The strength of a nation is reflected within all-round development of the children, who are destined to be successful citizens of tomorrow. Children should live with dignity. Their views should be listened to and respected in the same way as those of adults. The prosperity of nation does not depend on gigantic buildings and material resources but on human resources. There is also widespread acceptance, in principle, that children are entitled to fulfilment of their social and economic rights as well as special protection. Childhood is entitled to special care and assistance and children should grow up in an atmosphere of happiness, love and understanding. The concept of child is peculiar in Indian society in the sense that its cultural ethos is linked to the property of the family and the religious truth of continuation of family life. Society recognised children as potential citizen with right and duties but in need of special protection on account of their vulnerability. Society also expects parents to provide this care and protection. The Convention also recognises the exceptional vulnerability of children and it is guided by the principle of a first call of children. It obligates the State to respect and ensure that children get a fair and equitable deal in society and it is a means of empowering children and creating an environment in which the children are able to live securely and realise their full potentiality in life. Children are the foundation of a nation and the future course of progress is determined by their physical and mental well being which depend on their "right to survival, protection, development and participation is to protect and promote the well being of the children" in the society.

Concept of Child Abuse

In the wake of industrialization, urbanisation, socio-cultural transformation, eroded value system, disintegration of families, wide spread poverty and inequalities and lastly rapid growth of population, physical and mental hardships and exploitation of minors especially in the metropolis also contributed substantially to this serious problem. It enlightened the present form of rights in so far as it relates to child abuse. Kofi Annan the then Secretary General of the United Nations pointed out in his views "To look into some aspects of the future, we do not need projections by super computers. Much of the next millennium can be seen in how we care for our children today". Tomorrow's world may be influenced by science and technology, but more than anything, it is already taking shape in the bodies and minds of our children. It explicitly specifies the duty of mankind in discharging their responsibility towards the promotion and protection of the rights of the children in their future well-being.

Child abuse is a phenomenon that has existed as long as families have existed. Child abuse is a concept, which has emerged with the evolution of civilization. 'Child abuse' can be defined as causing or permitting any harmful or offensive contact on a child's body; and, any communication or transaction of any kind which humiliates, shames, or frightens the child. Verbal abuse and physical abuse in the name of discipline is common in India.

There is no standard definition on child abuse. However, it can be defined "Anything which individuals, institutions, or processes do (acts) or fail (omissions) to do which directly or indirectly harms children or damages the prospects of safe and healthy development into adulthood". Child abuse is shrouded in secrecy and there is a conspiracy of silence around the entire subject.

Definition of Child Abuse

The term 'Child Abuse' may have different connotations in different cultural milieu and socio-economic situations. A universal definition of child abuse in the Indian context does not exist and has yet to be defined. A narrow definition is limited to life threatening physical violence, including severe beatings, burns, exploitation and child labour. A broader definition includes any treatment other than the most favourable care and includes neglect, sexual or emotional abuse and exploitation. A child of any age, sex, race, religion, and socio-economic background can fall victim to child abuse, neglect and maltreatment. Neglect can be physical, educational, or emotional. Physical neglect includes not providing adequate food or clothing, appropriate medical care, supervision, or proper weather protection (heat or cold). It may include abandonment. Educational neglect includes failure to provide appropriate schooling or special educational needs, allowing excessive truancies. Psychological neglect includes the lack of any emotional support and love and never attending to the child.

Forms of Child Abuse

The forms of abuse are reflected in various reports about violence. But it is a crucial aspect to draw keen attention about what type of Violence and how many types of violence that exist in the society. These could be analysed in broader aspects, according to the context as three types of abuses which are generally occur in the society, *i.e. (i)* self-directed abuse, *(ii)* inter-personal abuse and *(iii)* collective abuse. These are enumerated below:

- *Self-directed Abuse:* Refers to violence where the perpetrator and the victim are the same person. It is subdivided into self-abuse and suicide.

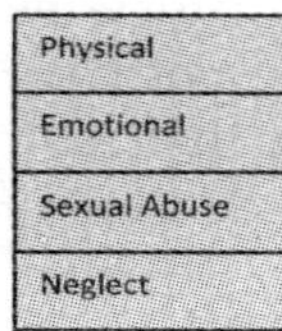

Fig. 1.1

- *Interpersonal Abuse:* Refers to violence between individuals. The category is subdivided into family and intimate partner violence, and community violence. The former includes child maltreatment, intimate partner violence and elder abuse. Community violence is broken down into violence by acquaintances and violence by strangers. It covers youth violence, assault by strangers, violence related to property crimes, and violence in workplaces and other institutions.
- *Collective Abuse:* Refers to violence committed by larger groups of people and can be subdivided into social, political and economic violence. The nature of acts can be physical, sexual, emotional or psychological, or one of neglect. The classification of violence according to both type and nature of the violent act provides a useful framework for understanding the place of child maltreatment within the complex patterns of violence.

Child abuse is very widespread and familiar phenomenon and a shocking characteristic of modern world. In today's scenario, it has become a very common incident when the innocent, defenceless, helpless child goes through physical, sexual and emotional abuse or even up to death. The effects of this trauma can be very deep and can last for life long period, which destroys the very roots of his or her physical and mental makeup. Thorough studies have shown that negligence and emotional abuse of child, which is so common every day, leaves much deeper impact on his/her mind than of physical abuse. According to World Health Organization the abuses are physical, sexual, emotional, neglect and commercial abuse.

- *Physical Abuse:* Physical abuse is the inflicting of physical injury upon a child. This may include burning, hitting, punching, shaking, kicking, beating or otherwise harming a child. The parent or caretaker may not have intended to hurt the child. It may, however, be the result of over-discipline or physical punishment that is inappropriate to the child's age.
- *Sexual Abuse:* Sexual abuse is inappropriate sexual behaviour with a child. It includes fondling a child's genitals, making the child fondle the adult's genitals, intercourse, incest, rape, sodomy, exhibitionism and sexual exploitation. To be considered 'child abuse', these acts have to be committed by a person responsible for the care of a child (for example a baby-sitter, a parent, or a daycare provider), or related to the child. If a stranger commits these acts, it would be considered sexual assault and handled solely by the police and criminal courts.
- *Emotional Abuse:* Emotional abuse is also known as verbal abuse, mental abuse, and psychological maltreatment. It includes acts or the failures to act by parents or caretakers that have caused or could cause, serious behavioural, cognitive, emotional, or mental trauma. This can include parents/caretakers using extreme and/or bizarre forms of punishment, such as confinement in a closet or dark room or being tied to a chair for long periods of time or

threatening or terrorizing a child. Less severe acts, but no less damaging, are belittling or rejecting treatment, using derogatory terms to describe the child, habitual tendency to blame the child or make him/her a scapegoat.

- *Neglect:* It is the failure to provide for the child's basic needs. Neglect can be physical, educational, or emotional. Physical neglect can include not providing adequate food or clothing, appropriate medical care, supervision, or proper weather protection (heat or cold). It may include abandonment. Educational neglect includes failure to provide appropriate schooling or special educational needs, allowing excessive truancies. Psychological neglect includes the lack of any emotional support and love and never attending to the child.
- *Commercial Abuse:* This refers to use of a child in activities that are meant for the benefit of others. It includes, but is not limited to, child labour and child prostitution. These activities are detrimental to the child's physical or mental health, educational, or spiritual, moral, social and emotional development.

A new front for child abuse emerged in tourist spots and pilgrims centres are spread across India. These are emerging as notorious hubs of unabated sexual abuse of minors and children. Tourism industry has grown worldwide and especially in developing countries, as a part and parcel of globalisation. Tourists come to the developing countries from different parts of the world for easy and cheap sexual gratification especially with children. The HIV/AIDS pandemic are having a devastating effect on children. This includes the 13 million children orphaned by AIDS, nearly 600,000 infants are infected every year through mother-to-child transmission and the millions of HIV-positive young people are living with this stigma. In number of other areas, some of them are more sensitive. It is pity to highlight here that, in the year 2008 review of child pornography laws with in 187 countries by the International Centre for Missing and Exploited Children (ICMEC) shows that 93 countries have no laws that specifically address child pornography, rest of that 94 that do but 36 do not criminalize the possession of child pornography. The conflation of trafficking with migration has brought forth many undesirable consequences. Trafficking is essentially a labour problem for it is done for placing of holding a person, where most of these people work without pay or on a low pay in bad conditions of work, with poor health and safety measures. A vibrant judicial system is a hall mark of greatness of any nation. The judiciary in India is acclaimed all over the world for its realistic and dynamic approach. It has identified the basic issues keeping in view the social objectives of our Constitution. Our Constitution not only assumes political justice but also social and economic justice. Effective access to justices can thus be seen as the most basic requirements and most basic human rights of the society.

Child abuse is a violation of the basic human rights of a child and is an outcome of a set of inter-related familial, social, psychological and economic factors. The problem of child abuse and human rights violations is one of the most critical matters on the international human rights agenda. In the Indian context, acceptance of child rights as primary inviolable rights is fairly recent, as is the universal understanding of it. The problem of child abuse and human rights violations is one of the most critical matters on the international human rights agenda. Physical of a child is the most inhuman act of aggression and an intrusion into the privacy of a child and a violation of his/her right to be respected, protected and loved as well as of her freedom of life. In addition, it examines two aspects and these are: *(i)* Strategies to address the problem of child abuse and *(ii)* Identification of areas of further research, based on the findings of the study. There are many factors that may contribute to the occurrence of child abuse and neglect. Child abuse and maltreatment is a complex issue. The survey is covered to various States including Orissa and as per the findings two out of every three children were physically abused. Every second child (both boys are girls) is reported to be facing emotional abuse.

In India, the only information available annually is the crime data maintained by NCRB, which records are only those crimes that can be registered under the IPC or other Criminal Acts. Corporal Punishment, use of children for creation of pornography, exposure, etc., are not reflected in NCRB data because those are not offences under the IPC. In India we are in conflict with none reporting and don't understand as offence and most of the time non-reporting occurs fear of reprisals by perpetrators, or of interventions by authorities which may worsen their overall situation. There is a gross under-reporting of crimes against children, which in itself is indicative of the low priority accorded to children by parents, caregivers and the police. The latest data of NCRB on different forms of child abuse is presented below in a graphical form:

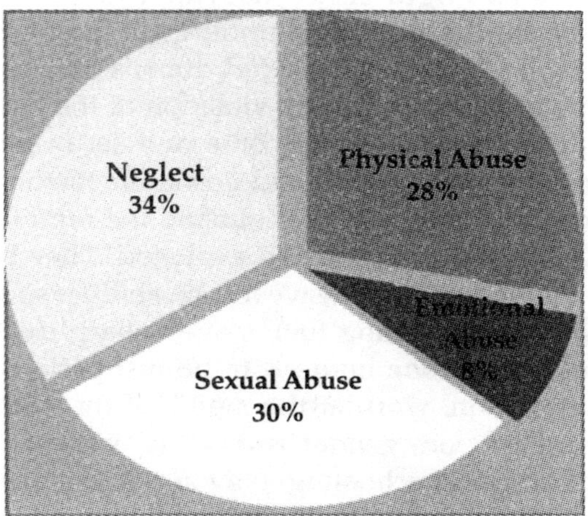

Fig. 1.2

Contributing Factors of Child Abuse

In the region of Asia, where population density is high, the issues of child labour and child sexual exploitation are also high. Political instability and other internal disturbances, including conditions of insurgency in many countries in Asia are also creating major problems, with increasing number of child soldiers, refugee children, trafficked children and children on the streets. There is a large child population in India and a large percentage of this population is vulnerable to abuse, exploitation and neglect. There is also inadequate information about the extent of child abuse in the country, No country can measure the extent and magnitude of the problem and progress towards the elimination. It is an urgent need to strengthen and integrate their strategies and measures for reducing the number of vulnerable children in accordance to law. The existence of the problem of child abuse in the study area is directly the outcome of the economic compulsions and is also because of lack of motivation on the part of the parents to send their child to school which is also an important factor to literate the kid and the society. One thing is essential here to note that everywhere, at every minute child abuse takes place. Problems might seem insurmountable. Forms and dynamics of child abuse have undergone major changes in recent decades, adding many sided dimensions, complexities and challenges. Child abuse is a violation of the basic 'human rights of a child' and is an outcome of a set of inter-related familial, social, psychological and economic factors. Children who work as domestic workers outside the family home are amongst the most vulnerable and exploited. They begin work at an early age, shoulder excessive responsibilities such as caring for babies/infants, handling fuel, stoves, sharp tools amongst others, working for long hours with no rest period, with little or no remuneration, work at the mercy of the employer and frequently suffer from gender and sexual violence. They are deprived of access of schooling, play and social activities and the affection and support of their family and friends". These situations or conditions not only apply to child domestic workers but also to all children at work. The Child Labour (Prohibition and Regulation) Act was enacted in 1986, to specifically address the situation of children in labour. However, this law distinguishes between hazardous and non-hazardous forms of labour, and identifies certain processes and occupations from which children are prohibited from working. It leaves out a large range of activities that children are engaged in and are exploited and abused. The large-scale exploitation and abuse of children employed in domestic work and hotels are cases in point. Child trafficking is one of the most heinous manifestations of violence against children. This is taking on alarming proportions – nationally and internationally. Although, very little reliable data or documentation is available, meetings and consultations across the country have revealed the gravity and the extent of this crime. It is high time we understood and realised that children are trafficked for a number of reasons and this cannot be treated synonymously with prostitution. The absence of this comprehensive understanding and a comprehensive law that addresses all forms of trafficking to back it makes this issue even more critical.

Preventive Measures on Child Abuse

The most serious challenge in preventing child abuse is the provision of basic needs for the survival, growth and development of children. Child abuse prevention must be oriented by the satisfaction of the child's needs in their socio-cultural context, and always based on a thorough knowledge of the variable aspects too. For the protection and prevention, the Constitution of India guarantees all children certain rights, which have been specially included for them as such in articles 14 and 15. Article, 21-A prescribes free and compulsory education for all children of the age of 6 to 14 years.

The Fundamental Rights embodied in Part-III and Directive Principles of State Policy enshrined in Part-IV of the Indian Constitution. It provides thorough framework for child rights. Several laws and national policies have been framed to implement the commitment to child rights. The State is required to ensure protection of children of tender age from abuse, and from entering vocations unsuited to their age and strength. But in poor families where economically backward parents forcibly send their children to work in order to supplement the income of the family, the children may never get any opportunity for enjoyment in their lives. The most precious and beautiful things in world is humble life. Therefore it is to be ensured that the children are treated humanely. The problem of child abuse and the network of its human rights violation hug some of the most dangerous aspects of the worst forms of child exploitation and abuse on the international human rights agenda. The U.N. Convention on the Rights of Child, 1989 is the most important instrument in the history of child rights at the international level and India ratified the Convention in 1992. The four major Articles pertaining to child abuse and neglect in the Convention are: Article 3: Protect the best interests of children; Article 19: Protect children from all forms of physical or mental violence, injury or abuse, neglect or negligent treatment, maltreatment or exploitation, including sexual abuse while in the care of parents, legal guardians or any person in whose care they are; Article 34: Undertake to protect children from all forms of sexual exploitation and sexual abuse; Article 35: Take all appropriate national, bilateral and multilateral measures to prevent the abduction of, sale of or traffic in children for any purpose or in any form. The CRC requires States should be concerned to prevent all forms of violence and to respond to violence effectively when it occurs. While the State cannot be held directly responsible for individual acts of violence against children by parents or others, it is required to provide a framework of law and other necessary measures to supply adequate protection, including effective deterrence. Few States have put in place the necessary laws prohibiting all violence against children, together with policies, structures, and reporting and referral mechanisms to address violence in the home and family. Law enforcement officials in many countries remain reluctant to intervene even in cases of severe violence, child marriage, and incest. Violent forms of discipline remain legal and socially accepted in many States, despite the consistent interpretation of the CRC and other human rights instruments as requiring their prohibition and elimination (most recently, this has been underlined by the Committee's General Comment No. 8, 2006 on "The right of the child to protection from corporal punishment and other cruel or degrading forms of punishment.

The judges of the Supreme Court must not merely isolate themselves in an ivory tower and neglect the needs and problems that plague our society. It is commonly marked by decisions calling for social engineering and occasionally the decisions represent intrusions in the legislative and executive matters.

In the past six decades Indian Judiciary have done a marvellous job in protecting right, liberty, dignity, and the Rule of Law against all obnoxious odds by controlling the abuse of administrative discretions and arbitrary actions. Laws cannot be enforced in the absence of a favourable consensus. A strong will to uplift the plight of the child coupled with strong legislative and legal measures will improve the situation.

Review of Literature

Though research in the field of child abuse is of recent development yet a plethora of literature has been mounted in this short span of time to prove the growing interest of the scholars in this field. In order to give a definite direction as well as sound theoretical base to the present study, it is imperative to take a dip into it to unfolded manifold trends and traits of studies, which are taken up.

Segal in his article assessed the attitudes and perceptions of child abuse in India among urban professionals. His findings were preliminary, because the sample size was small and non-random. Generalised results indicated that some human services professionals were no more or less sensitive than the untrained to the effects of abusive behaviour. Comparisons with other studies, such as those by Giovannoni and Becerra, indicate a strong cultural context, which makes transportation of intervention and training across national boundaries questionable. He was of the opinion that the Indian view holds the child as parental property, subject to discipline as parents find appropriate. Battering of children in India is not seen as detrimental to the child, as it is in the U.S. Definitions of child abuse in India need to be operationalised. An instrument developed by Giovannoni and Becerra consists of 78 vignette pairs which depict child maltreatment in 13 areas: cleanliness, clothing, drugs/alcohol, educational neglect, emotional neglect, fostering delinquency, housing, medical neglect, nutrition, parental sexual norms, physical abuse, sexual abuse, and supervision. In India sample of 133 social workers, human services professionals, and nonhuman service professionals from Delhi, Bombay, and Hyderabad completed questionnaires, which included the scaled evaluation of 63 vignettes of abusive behaviour by parents. Maltreatment of children in India was identified as:

1. Societal abuse.
2. Physical maltreatment.
3. Sexual abuse.
4. Non-physical maltreatment.

The analysis focused on stem vignettes, because 'consequences' to the child were problematic. Child prostitution was considered the most serious offense and poor housing conditions the least. Differences were found between professional groups for all areas except child prostitution and sexual abuse. Comparisons were also made to U.S., findings in 1979. In the Indian sample, the perceived seriousness varied with the nature of the abuse.

Arlene Manoharan in his work titled "A Critique of the Juvenile Justice Act 2000 in the context of the adoption issue" opined that: Adoption is dealt with under Section 41 of the Juvenile Justice Act, 2000 (JJ Act), which outlines provisions for the social integration and rehabilitation of children coming under the Act. The present study covered positive features of adoption under JJ Act 2000 and limitations of the JJ Act. It was observed that JJ Act empowers the Child Welfare Board (CWB) to give a child in adoption and requires the child's consent before adoption, when the child is able to understand and express his/her consent. JJ Act was silent on the issue of grandchildren. The Act was silent on the question of religion, which implied that persons of any religion can adopt a child of any religion. However, a closer look at the legalities may reveal limitations in this regard. It was revealed that in JJ Act 2000 there was no definition of adoption. There was no clarity as to whether there is a possibility of re-adoption of an adopted child if he/she is once again abandoned or orphaned, or whether the first adoption itself is irrevocable. Inter-country adoptions also came under the purview of the Guardians and Wards Act and hence no placement is possible under the JJ Act 2000. Another limitation was to recognise all children's homes and State government institutions for orphans as adoption agencies. It was recommended that the provisions for adoption under the JJ Act 2000 would need to be challenged. The Act fails to provide the much needed secular, child rights centric, gender justice and enabling options that is the need of the hour. The immediate solution would be to push for an enabling legislation such as Special Adoption Act. Though this process would undoubtedly take time, it is not in the interest of children, prospective adoptive parents or genuine adoption agencies to push unresolved adoption issues through back door legislation such as JJ Act 2000. Moreover, this hegemonic approach itself needs to be challenged so that democratic, people oriented processes ultimately take precedence over the hasty political manipulations of those who have drafted and enacted this legislation without adequate basic policy clarity.

Deepti Pagare, *et al.* (2004) in their study "Sexual abuse of street children brought to an observation home" observed that WHO estimates that globally 8 per cent boys and 25 per cent girls below age 18 suffer sexual abuse of some kind every year. Sexual abuse of children in India occurs across all socio-economic classes and is widespread among boys and girls, both in rural and urban areas. Perpetrators of sexual abuse find their victims in wide ranging situations, and homeless boys, living in an unprotected environment on streets; make easy prey for sexual abuse. The study was conducted at an Observation Home for Boys in Delhi where non-delinquent male juveniles aged 6-18 years are temporarily detained. All the boys admitted for the first time to the Observation Home between May to October 2002 were included. The boys were requested to undergo examination in a separate room by the Medical Officer, based on the Guidelines of American Medical Association (AMA, 1985) for Primary Care Physicians for diagnosis of suspected sexual abuse. All the boys were assured confidentiality and none was forced to undergo physical examination against his will. A total of 202 boys were willing for clinical examination, but the final sample consisted of 189 boys. Among the 178 subjects living away from families, 62.9 per cent had left home between 6 to 10 years of age. Overall, 38.1 per cent boys reported sexual abuse, with use of force ranging from 4.8 per cent to 23.8 per cent. Over 15 per cent boys reported penetrative sexual abuse. The maximum proportion of abuse was reported in the age group of 8-10 years (42.9%). The mean age at abuse was reported as 9.13 + 2.4 years. Most children (93.2%) reported the incident to be within 2-3 weeks of leaving home. All boys reported single episode of sexual abuse except four. The maximum proportion of incidents occurred during late evening or at night (59.2%). 22.2 per cent cases occurred during the day. Most children (76.2%) were abused at railway stations, about 4 per cent were abused at the work place and 1.4 per cent at some other Observation Homes. Among the 72 abused children, 44 (61.1%) had some physical sign of abuse while 29 (40.2%) showed behavioural signs of sexual abuse. 18 boys had signs suggestive of sexually transmitted diseases, and this also increased their vulnerability to HIV infection. The problem of sexual abuse among inmates of Observation Homes is grave and requires urgent remedial action. The period of detention at Observation Homes may be utilised for identification of the victims and their proper medical, social and psychological rehabilitation to prevent further abuse. Concerned authorities should take appropriate action and make efforts to create safe living conditions for all children, including street children.

Seva Mandir, Udaipur conducted a study titled 'Abuse of Children' in 2005. The major findings are as follows: Child abuse is both shocking and common place. Child abusers inflict physical, sexual and emotional trauma on defenseless children every day. The present study was undertaken to find out the incidence of child abuse in schools. The study also reveals the probable reasons for child abuse, and suggests ways that can help Seva Mandir in preventing occurrence of child abuse. The study was carried out in 3 villages of Kherwara block in Udaipur district. Data was collected using a self-designed questionnaire administered to the sample surveyed, unobtrusive observation of children, and visit to schools. A mix of quota and snowball sampling technique was used. Parents of 84 per cent children were satisfied with the level of their performance. The use of a stick to correct the faults of children was considered right by 96 per cent parents, while 20 per cent parents said that they would do nothing to correct the situation. Only 6 per cent parents believed that they should go to the teacher and converse with them. 47 per cent students stated that they became fearful when they thought about their teachers. 40 per cent of the students became very uncomfortable when they thought about their teachers. 93 per cent students confirmed that they felt very happy going to school. When asked which animal would best represent their teacher, 57 per cent of the respondents chose the picture of a black cobra, 14 per cent a black panther, 10 per cent a tiger, and 20 per cent a beautiful horse. Parents can play a major role in determining the degree of abuse a child is subjected to. If the parents continue to believe that physically abusing the child is a necessary part of education, then very little can be done to prevent the incidences of child abuse. There is need to make parents aware of the rights of the child to a life without abuse, and parents should delay their need for personal gratification from the child. Teachers should be aware of alternative means of establishing discipline among students. Parents must be made aware of the need for a healthy atmosphere at home for the complete development of the child. There is also a need to involve the common man in all these efforts.

Centre for the Prevention and Healing of Child Sexual Abuse, Chennai conducted a study on "Prevalence and dynamics of child sexual abuse among school going children in Chennai" in (2006). Child sexual abuse is a well kept secret in India, and in society there is ignorance, denial and silence about the issue. The present study was done with an objective to assess the prevalence and dynamics of child sexual abuse among school going children of 11th Standard in Chennai. 24 schools were taken covering 2211 students, of whom 847 were boys and 1364 were girls. Data were collected from the children using a self-reported anonymous questionnaire. The key indicators used in the study were sex, age, family type, family income, and school type. Results showed that out of a total of 2211 children, 939 (42%) had faced sexual abuse. There was a myth in society that boys were not sexually abused, but data showed that sexual abuse was higher among boys (48%) than girls (39%). Results contradicted various other myths. There was a general perception that sexual abuse was extremely common among poor and illiterate families. But the study found that prevalence of child sexual abuse in upper and middle class was proportionately higher than that in lower and lower middle class. Sexual abuse was found to be higher in joint families (335/413) as compared to nuclear families (589/814). The most prevalent forms of sexual abuse were touching children's private parts, exhibitionism, forcing and/or tricking children to watch pornography. Prevalence of severe forms of sexual abuse was found to be 21 per cent among boys and 15 per cent among girls. Frequency of abuse was 'do not remember' 43 per cent, once 34 per cent, more than 5 times 7 per cent, and 2-5 times 16 per cent. Those who were abused once were abused mainly by strangers, whereas those who were abused repeatedly were abused by people whom they were familiar with. The age of 11-15 years was the age of onset of abuse for most girls and boys. The most common tactics used by abusers were force, trickery, blackmail, gifts and intimidation. Out of a total of 939 children who reported to have been abused, only 360 had ever sought help. The study showed that most abused children disclosed the abuse to their friends and then their mothers. It was found that a large number of children wanted information on how to protect themselves against sexual abuse. More importantly, prevention, through the concept of Personal Safety Education empowers every child to exercise the right to be safe all the time, and it strengthens the ability of all those morally and socially responsible for the protection of children, that is the State, parents, other significant stakeholders and the larger community.

Harish Joshi and others in their study entitled 'Children without Childhood' have stated that a street child is a global urban phenomenon and their number is increasing. Among them, the children who have run away from their homes and are struggling for survival on their own, and those who have no families are the most vulnerable. This study was conducted in response to a need expressed at a large GO-NGO meeting in Ahmedabad to discuss child rights. This study endeavours to bring to light some details of the lives of these vulnerable street children so that those working with them get clues to devise their strategies for operation. The study was conducted at the main Kalupur Railway Station and under the nearby Sarangpur bridge, 153 street children were interviewed to find out the reasons for leaving home, place of stay, duration of stay, occupations followed, earning and expenditure, harassment, treatment of sickness, willingness to study and feelings about being away from homes and family members. For the in-depth study 34 street children were interviewed. NGO officials, hotel owners where street children went for meals, owners of food stalls at Kalupur Railway Station, and traders who were contact with these children cast insight on this issue.

They opined that the legislation to become effective, measures encompassing education, employment and income generation, social strata and child development must accompany it. The phenomenon of street children cannot be eliminated in a short spell of time. The focus also has to be on improving the living conditions of Scheduled Caste and protecting them from exploitation for which well co-ordinated and committed efforts are required.

The Study on Child Abuse: India 2007 done by the Ministry of Women and Child Development, Government of India, is a bold and commendable initiative. The study aimed to develop a comprehensive understanding of child abuse with a view to facilitating the formulation of appropriate policies and programmes and thereby curbing child abuse in India. The research was done across 13 States and it involved 2,447 children, 2,324 young adults, and 2,449 stakeholders. Children in the family environment, in school, at work, on the streets, and in institutions were interviewed. Different forms of child abuse – physical, sexual, emotional, and neglect of the girl child – were studied. The major results were as follows: children in the 5-12 age group are most at risk of different kinds of abuse and exploitation; two out of three children were physically abused; 53.2 per cent of children reported having faced one of more forms of sexual abuse, with 21.9 per cent facing severe forms of sexual abuse; and 5.7 per cent of the respondents reported being sexually assaulted. Street children, children at work, and children in institutional care were found to be particularly vulnerable to sexual assault. Every second child reported facing emotional abuse, and 48.4 per cent of respondents who were girls wished that they were boys. For a large number of children reporting abuse of any form, parents and those in a position of trust and responsibility were the abusers. Most children did not disclose the matter to anyone. The States of Andhra Pradesh, Assam, Bihar, and Delhi reported higher rates of abuse of all forms as compared to other States.

The Bureau of Police Research and Development, New Delhi conducted a study entitled 'Child Abuse: An Overview'. The major findings include: Around 40 million children under the age of 14 years are estimated to suffer from abuse and neglect around the world. The prevalence of child abuse is showing an increasing trend in India. India has a large child population and many children are vulnerable to abuse, exploitation and neglect. The present study assessed the inter-connected factors associated with child abuse to develop a comprehensive understanding of the phenomenon; evaluated the magnitude and forms of child abuse; aimed to sensitize the public about the serious danger of prevalence of child abuse, especially child sexual abuse in society; assessed the existing legal framework to deal with the problem; and attempted to draw inferences from a national study titled 'Study on Child Abuse: India 2007' undertaken by Prayas Institute of Juvenile Justice. The survey was carried out across 13 States and covered a sample size of 12,447 children. It was observed that there were many definitions of child abuse but the originally used definition "Acts or omissions by a care given leading to actual or potential damage to health and development, and exposure to unnecessary suffering to the child" was quite appropriate. It was found that younger children, 5-12 years of age, reported higher level of abuse. Boys, as compared to girls, were equally at risk of abuse, and persons in trust and authority were major abusers. 70 per cent of the abused child respondents never reported the matter to anyone. It was observed that two out of every three children were physically abused. Out of 69 per cent children who were physically abused in 13 sample States, 54.68 per cent were boys. It was found that over 50 per cent children in the entire 13 sample States were being subjected to one or the other forms of physical abuse, 88.6 per cent were physically abused by parents, 65 per cent school going children reported facing corporal punishment, and 50.2 per cent children worked 7 days a week. 53.22 per cent children reported that they faced one or more forms of sexual abuse, and 21.9 per cent children reported facing severe forms of sexual abuse. Children in Assam, Andhra Pradesh, Bihar and Delhi reported the highest incidence of sexual assault. In 83 per cent cases parents were the abusers and 48.4 per cent girls wished they were boys. The study on child sexual abuse conducted among 2211 students (847 boys and 1364 girls) from schools in Chennai Corporation zone revealed that 939 children had faced at least one form of sexual abuse at some point of time, and 48 per cent of the boys had been abused. The forms of sexual abuse prevalent were touching children's private parts (603), exhibitionism (384), forcing or tricking children to watch pornography (371), making children touch the offender's private parts (226), made to remove clothes (83), oral sex (131), and sexual intercourse (81). From the above it was concluded that sexual abuse is one of the most fundamental violations of children's rights, and was usually an underlying obstacle to their overall development. It was recommended that the present National Policy on Children, 1974 needed to be revised, and a mechanism created which may include child care and protection at village, block, district and State levels. This mechanism may involve parents, elected representatives of urban and rural local bodies, teachers, *anganwadi* workers, medical practitioners, police and social workers, and responsible members of the public among others. Media should be used to spread awareness on child rights. School teachers need to be trained to handle misbehaving students through guidance and counselling. Stringent laws should be enacted to completely curb child abuse and sex tourism in the country.

2 The Causes of Child Abuse

Child abuse has for a long-time been recorded in literature, art and science in many parts of the world. Report on infanticide, mutilation, abandonment and other forms of violence against children dates back to ancient civilization. From the very inception of civilization people have realised that proper child development was the key to their perpetuation. The significance and the importance of the child lie in the fact that the child is the universe. If there was no child, there would be no humanity and there cannot be universe without humanity. Child is a bud, it nourishes in this conducive environment. It is not an exaggeration to say that the children are the blooming flowers of garden of society and so it is our duty to protect these flowers from damaging effects of excessive exposure to heat, cold, and rain etc. Children are valuable asset and indeed they are the building blocks of nations and all of humanity. Social Justice must begin with children. The tender plant is until unless properly nourished, it has little chances for growing into a strong useful tree. Social justice in the scale of first priority will be given for the welfare of the children. Community welfare strengthens social and economic development. Children's are people live with dignity. Their views should be listened to and respected in the same way as those of adults. The prosperity of nation does not depend on gigantic buildings and material resources but on human resources. There is also widespread acceptance, in principle, that children are entitled to fulfilment of their social and economic rights as well as special protection. Childhood is entitled to special care and assistance and children should grow up in an atmosphere of happiness, love and understanding. It has played an important role in promoting children as a priority in the making of the public policy, not just in the developing world but also in the rich countries. Every child has the right to life and free from violence. The Convention also recognises the exceptional vulnerability of children and it is guided by the principle of a first call of children. It obligates the state to respect and ensure that children get a fair and equitable deal in society and it is a means of empowering children and creating an environment in which the children are able to live securely and realise their full potentiality in life. Children's are the foundation of a nation and the future course of progress is determined by their physical and mental well being which depend on their "right to survival, protection, development and participation is the need of hour to protect and promote the well being of the children" in the society.

Each and every year millions of children around the world are victimized. It witnesses various abuses as physical, sexual and emotional abuse. Child abuse and neglect is a huge global problem in these days. It creates a serious impact on the development of Childs physical and mental health throughout their lives and also society in general. This chapter exclusively focuses on the causes that are responsible for the abuse of a child. For which he may face the dire consequences. In this myriad aspect an attempt is made to asses the magnitude causes and forms of child abuse, its effect and consequences enshrined in the society. Child abuse is a term that generally refers to mistreatment of a child by parent or another adult. There is no standard factor responsible for child abuse. A narrow definition is limited to life threatening physical violence, including sever beatings. A broader definition includes any treatment other then the most favourable care. No one knows how many instances of child abuse occur each year, because of child abuse are never reported. However, the national care for child abuse and neglect estimates that millions of children suffer non-accident life threatening physical violence each year. Child abuse gained major public attention in India during 1980, but the causes have changed more often the years. Each year, tens of thousands of children are traumatized by physical, sexual, and emotional abusers or by caregivers who neglect them, making child abuse as common as it is shocking. With the progress of Industrialization, there is an increasing tendency to reduce working cost to make quick profits. It has aggravated the exploitative practice and social evil and employment of children has become a common practice in worldwide. It is quite unfortunate to describe here that two-thirds of children are undernourished, their minds and bodies growing less than their God-given and genetic potential. Some 25 million young children are not enrolled in school and an equal number drop out before attaining even the basic skills of reading and writing. Twenty million or more are fully engaged in the labour force, having virtually no childhood worthy of the name of 300 million Indian. Children, boys outnumber girls by nearly eight million, two-thirds of out of school children's are girls, as majority of children in hazardous workplaces are again, girls. Small wonder, ears often greet the birth of a girl child.

Today, research has shown, many experts opines, child abuse is widespread because society regards physical punishment by parents as a reasonable way of changing children's behaviours. Most of us can't imagine what would make adult to use violence against a child, and the worse the behaviour is, the more unimaginable it seems. But the incidence of parent's and other caregivers consciously, even wilfully, committing acts that harm to every child. They're supposed to be nurturing is a sad fact of human society that cuts across all lines of ethnicity and class. Whether the abuse is rooted in the perpetrator's mental illness, substance abuse, or inability to cope, the psychological result for each abused child is often the same: deep emotional scars and a feeling of worthlessness. Child violence often occurs alongside other types of violence. For instance, child abuse by adults within the family is frequently found in the same settings as intimate partner violence.

Neglected children are themselves at increased risk in later life of either perpetrating or becoming the victims of multiple types of violence – including suicide, sexual violence, youth violence, intimate partner violence and child maltreatment. The same set of factors such as harmful levels of alcohol use, family isolation and social exclusion, high unemployment, and economic inequalities have been shown to underlie the different types of violence.

The scars can be deep and long lasting, affecting not just abused children but society. Another common view is that abused children grown-up to be abusive adults, a development referred to as the cycle of abuse. Many types of abuses are comes to lime light but the main factors contribute a lot about the abuse.

It is learnt that the signs and symptoms of child abuse and find out where to get help for the children and their caregivers. There are many forms of child abuse and they vary according to cultural and geographical settings. In this chapter, the researcher has tried her best to throw light on the following four prominent forms of child abuse and their causes.

Types of Abuses and Its Causes

There are four primary types of child abuses are:

1. Physical abuse.
2. Sexual abuse.
3. Emotional abuse.
4. Neglect.

While the first two categories get the most attention, perhaps because they involve physical violence, neglect is far and away upon the most common form of child abuse. In accountability more than 60 per cent of all cases are child maltreatment. Many abused children will suffer short or long-term psychological trauma. One type of abuse has received much attention in newspapers and television, children are warned not to let people, and even family members touch them in ways that makes them feel uncomfortable.

Physical Abuse

Physical abuse of a child is defined as the intentional use of physical force against a child that results in or has a high likelihood of resulting in harm for the child's health, survival, development or dignity. *Physical child abuse* is an adult's physical act of aggression directed at a child that causes injury, even if the adult didn't intend to injure the child. Such acts of aggression include striking a child with the hand, fist, or foot or with an object; burning the child with a hot object; shaking, pushing, or throwing a child; pinching or biting the child; pulling a child by the hair; cutting off a child's air. Such acts of physical aggression account for between 15 and 20 per cent of documented child abuse cases arose each year. Many physically abusive parents and caregivers insist that their actions are simply forms of discipline, ways to make children learn to behave. But there's a big difference between giving an unmanageable child a swat on the backside and twisting the child's arm until it breaks. Physically abusive parents have issues of anger, excessive need for control, or immaturity that make them unable or unwilling to see their level of aggression as inappropriate. Sometimes the very youngest children, even babies not yet born, suffer physical abuse. Because many chemicals passes easily to a pregnant woman's system into a foetus, if a mother consume drugs or alcohol during pregnancy can cause serious neurological and physiological damage to the unborn child. As such it affect as fatal alcohol syndrome; mother's breast milk also diluted with that drug and alcohol. A woman who drinks or uses drugs knowingly that she is pregnant could be charged with child abuse in many jurisdictions, if her baby is born with problems because of the substance use. Another form of child abuse involving babies is *shaken baby syndrome*, in which a frustrated caregiver shakes a baby roughly to make the baby stop crying. The baby's neck muscles can't support the baby's head yet, and the brain bounces around inside its skull, suffering damage that often leads to severe neurological problems and even death. While the person shaking the baby may not mean to hurt him, shaking a baby in a way that can cause injury is a form of child abuse. An odd form of physical child abuse is Munchausen's syndrome by proxy, in which a parent causes a child to become ill and rushes the child to the hospital or convinces doctors that the child is sick. It's a way for the parent to gain attention and sympathy, and its dangers to the child constitute child abuse. Corporal punishment is also physical abuse the use of physical force with the intent of inflicting bodily pain, but not injury, for the purpose of correction or control, used to be a very common form of discipline: most of us know it as spanking or paddling. And many of us were spanked as children without damage to body or psyche. The widespread use of physical punishment, however, doesn't make it a good idea. Most child-care experts have come to agree that corporal punishment sends the message to children that physical force is an appropriate response to problems or opposition. The level of force used by an angry or frustrated parent can easily get out of hand and lead to injury. Even if it doesn't, what a child learnt from being hit as right or wrong, than about behaving well or hiding bad behaviour out of fear of being hit. As signs of physical child abuse includes visible mark of maltreatment, such as cuts, bruises, welts, or well-defined burns, and reluctance to go home. If you ask a child about how he or she got hurt and the child talks vaguely or evasively about falling off a fence or spilling a hot dish, think hard before you accept the child's story at face value. The overall percentage of physical abuse was reported as 72 per cent from street children, working children, children at home and children in Institutions. These children were from different socio-economic backgrounds and more likely to face exploitation and abuse, there can be no doubt that the effect of hurt, pain, anger, humiliation and loss of self-esteem is enormous.

Sexual Abuse

Sexual abuse is defined as the involvement of a child in sexual activity that he or she does not fully comprehend, is unable to give informed consent to, or for which the child is not developmentally prepared, or else that violates the laws or social taboos of society. Both adults and other children, who are by virtue of their age or stage of development, can sexually abuse children in a position of responsibility, trust or power over the victim. It comes to limelight that, only 10 per cent abuses between an adult and child. Such acts include: *(a)* Behaviour involving penetration, *(b)* fondling, *(c)* Violation of privacy, *(d)* Exposing children to adult sexuality, *(e)* Exploitation in the form of selling child's services as a prostitute or a performer in pornography etc. The adult who sexually abuses a child or adolescent is usually someone the child knows and is supposed to trust: a relative, childcare provider, family friend, neighbour, teacher, coach, or clergy member. More than 80 per cent of sex offenders are people known person to the child or adolescent victims? It is important to understand that no matter what the adult says in defence of his or her actions, but the child did not invite the sexual activity rather adult's behaviour is wrong.

Sexual Abuse is Never the Child's Fault

Children are psychologically unable to handle sexual stimulation. Even toddlers, who haven't formulated the idea that the sexual abuse is wrong, will develop problems resulting from the over stimulation. Older children who know and care for their abusers know that the sexual behaviour is wrong, but they may feel trapped by feelings of loyalty and affection. Abusers warn their victims not to tell, threatening children with violence or ostracism, and the shame associated with the sexual activity makes the child especially reluctant to tell. When sexual abuse occurs within the family, children may worry that other family members won't believe them and will be angry with them if they tell – as is often the case. The layer of shame that accompanies sexual abuse makes the behaviour doubly traumatizing. Some signs of sexual child abuses are that, often children who have suffered sexual abuse show no physical signs, and the abuse goes undetected unless a physician spots evidence of forced sexual activity. However, there are behavioural clues to sexual abuse, including:

- Inappropriate interest in or knowledge of sexual acts.
- Seductive behaviour.
- Reluctance or refusal to undress in front of others.
- Extra aggression or, at the other end of the spectrum, extra compliance.
- Fear of a particular person or family member.
- Children who use the Internet are also vulnerable to come-ons by adults online. Among the warning signs of online sexual child abuse are these:
- Your child spends large amounts of time online, especially at night.
- You find pornography on your child's computer.
- Your child receives phone calls from people you don't know, or makes calls, sometimes long distance, to numbers you don't recognise.
- Your child receives mail, gifts, or packages from someone you don't know.
- Your child turns the computer monitor off or quickly changes the screen on the monitor when you come into the room.
- Your child becomes withdrawn from the family.
- Your child is using an online account belonging to someone else.

Emotional Abuse

Emotional and psychological abuse involves both isolated incidents, as well as a pattern of failure over time on the part of a parent or caregiver to provide a developmentally appropriate and supportive environment. Acts in this category may have a high probability of damaging the child's physical or mental health, or its physical, mental, spiritual, moral or social development. Abuse of this type includes: the restriction of movement; patterns of belittling, blaming, threatening, frightening, discriminating against or ridiculing; and other non-physical forms of rejection or hostile treatment. Emotional child abuse and the types as well as warning signs are discussed below:

Emotional child abuse involves behaviour that interferes with a child's mental health or social development: one website calls it 'the systematic tearing down of another human being'. Such abuse can range from verbal insults to acts of terror, and it's almost always a factor in the other three categories of abuse. While emotional abuse by itself doesn't involve the infliction of physical pain or inappropriate physical contact, it can have more long-lasting negative psychological effects than either physical abuse or sexual abuse. Emotional abuse is quite different in its broader aspects includes:

(a) Verbal abuse.

(b) Withholding affection.

(c) Extreme punishment.

(d) Corruption, etc.

(a) *Verbal Abuse*: Belittling or shaming the child, name calling, making negative comparisons to others, telling the child he or she is no good, 'worthless' 'a mistake' or Habitual blaming-telling the child that everything is his or her fault.

(b) Ignoring or disregarding the child, due to lack of affection and warmth-failure to hug, praise, express love for the child.

(c) These are actions that are meant to isolate and terrorize a child, such as tying a child to a fixture or piece of furniture or locking a child in a closet or dark room.

(d) This involves causing a child to witness or participate in inappropriate behaviour such as criminal activities drug or alcohol abuse or acts of violence.

Emotional abuse can come not only from adults but also from other children: siblings, neighbourhood or schoolyard bullies, and peers in schools that permit a culture of social ostracism (the 'mean girl' syndrome. The signs of emotional child abuse include apathy, depression, and hostility. If it happens at school, the child may be reluctant to go to school and develop or fake a physical complaint.

Causes of Child Abuse

It is important to consider that both men and women can be neglectful or abusive towards children. Why would someone abuse a defenceless child? What kind of person abuses a child? Not all child abuse is deliberate or intended. Several factors in a person's life may combine to cause them to abuse a child. These are as follows:

- *Stress,* Including the stress of caring for children, or the stress of caring for a child with a disability, special needs, or difficult behaviours.
- Lack of nurturing qualities necessary for child care.
- *Immaturity:* A disproportionate number of parents who abuse their children are teenagers.
- Difficulty controlling anger.
- Personal history of being abused.
- Isolation from the family or community.
- Physical or mental health problems, such as depression and anxiety.
- Alcohol or drug abuse.
- Personal problems such as marital conflict, unemployment, or financial difficulties.

No one has been able to predict which of these factors will cause someone to abuse a child. A significant factor is that abuse tends to be *intergenerational* – those who were abused as children are more likely to repeat the act when they become parents or caretakers. In addition, many forms of child abuse arise from ignorance. Sometimes a cultural tradition leads to abuse. Such beliefs include:

A child is not a property, no-doubt that the Parents (especially father and mothers) have the right to control their children in any way they wish. Children need to be toughened up to face the hardships of life. Girls need to be genitally mutilated to assure virginity, it is often traumatic for the children.

Effects of Child Abuse

Child abuse can produce dire consequences during the victim's childhood and adulthood. Some effects of child abuse are obvious: a child is malnourished or has a cast on her arm; a nine-year-old develops a sexually transmitted disease. But some physiological effects of child abuse, such as cognitive difficulties or lingering health problems, may not show up for some time or be clearly attributable to abuse. Other effects of child abuse are invisible or go off like time bombs later in life.

Emotional Effects of Child Abuse

Emotional abuse plays a vital role in every type of abuses. Just as all types of child abuse has an emotional component, all affect the emotions of the victims. These effects include; Low self-esteem, Depression and anxiety, Aggressive behaviour/anger issues, Relationship difficulties, Alienation and withdrawal, personality disorders, clinginess, neediness, Flashback and nightmares. Many adults who were abused as children find it difficult to trust other people, endure physical closeness, and establish intimate relationships.

Behavioural Effects of Child Abuse is that, Child abuse can play itself out not only in how its victims feel but also in what they do years later. Children who suffer abuse have much greater chances of being arrested later as juveniles and as adults. Significant percentages come to accountability. One of every three abused or neglected children will grow up to become an abusive parent.

Other behavioural effects include: Problems in school and work, Prostitution, Teen Pregnancy, Suicide attempts, Criminal or antisocial behaviour, Alcohol and drug abuse, Eating disorders, Spousal abuse.

Although many people are reluctant to get involved in other families' lives, when it comes to child abuse, you don't have the option of keeping mum. If you know of a child being abused or even suspect abuse, you have the responsibility to report it. An outline of protective and preventive measures to check this rampant practice described in chapter-VI of this research paper.

Neglect

Neglect is the most prevalent form of abuse. Physical abuse is the second most prevalent form followed by sexual abuse. Maltreatment includes both isolated incidents, as well as a pattern of failure over time on the part of a parent or other family member to provide for the development and well-being of the child – where the parent is in a position to do so – in one or more of the areas as Health, education, development, nutrition, shelter and living conditions. The parents of neglected children are not necessarily poor. They may equally be financially well off but other factors are responsible too.

Causes of Neglect and Types of Warning Signs

Neglect is a pattern of failing to provide for a child's basic needs, to the extent that the child's physical and/or psychological well-beings are damaged or not to do their job.

There are three basic types of neglect. Failures to provide adequate food, clothing, or hygiene, the highlighted issues are:

Physical Neglect

- Reckless disregard for the child's safety, such as inattention to hazards in the home, drunk driving with kids in the car, leaving a baby unattended.
- Refusal to provide or delay in providing necessary health care for the child.
- Abandoning children without providing for their care or expelling children from the home without arranging the care.

Educational Neglect

These are the following educational neglects by which the child abuses:

- Failure to enrol a child in school.
- Permitting or causing a child misses too many days of school.
- Refusal to follow up on obtaining services for a child's special educational needs.

Emotional Neglect

- Due to inadequate nurturing or affection.
- Exposure, of the child to spousal abuse.
- Permitting a child to drink alcohol or use recreational drugs.
- Failure to intervene when the child demonstrates antisocial behaviours. Refusal of or delay in providing necessary psychological care.

Some Signs of Child Neglect

- Clothes that are dirty, ill-fitting, ragged, and/or not suitable for the weather.
- *Unwashed Appearance*: Offensive body odour.
- *Indicators of Hunger*: Asking for or stealing food, going through trash for food, eating too fast or too much when food is provided for a group.
- *Apparent Lack of Supervision:* Wandering alone, home alone, left in a car.
- Colds, fevers, or rashes left untreated; infected cuts; chronic tiredness.
- In school children, frequent absence or lateness; troublesome, disruptive behaviour or its opposite, withdrawal.
- In babies, failure to thrive; failure to relate to other people or to surroundings.
- A single occurrence of one of these indicators isn't necessarily a sign of child neglect, but a pattern of behaviours may demonstrate a lack of care that constitutes abuse.

Common Factors Responsible for Child Abuse

No single factor is responsible for child abuse or maltreatment but it is a collective and contributive factor for child abuse. At the same time no single factor on its own could explain why some individuals behave violently towards children or why child abuse appears to be more prevalent in certain communities than in others. Children living in poverty may be exposed to multiple risks and become vulnerable to exploitation, violence, discrimination and stigmatization. Gabriel de Trade the French Jurist and social psychologist provides the standing explanation of crime in term of social factor, according to him criminal behaviours in the result of a learning process. A person learns criminal behaviour just like any other trade, which he picks up in his childhood. Similarly many factors are there which are increase susceptibility towards child abuse are known as 'Risk factor' and some other factors are also decreasing susceptibility towards the protective factor. Simultaneously both the factors are working for child abuse in a society. Child abuse occurs in a society when the protective factor does not perform the responsibility or more crud and traditionally which itself create abuse, or as other forms of violence. Child abuse is best understood by analysing the complex interaction of a number of factors at different levels. It is to be vital to understand that to deals effectively with the problem of child abuse/neglect.

There are many factors, which create and enhanced the situation of child abuse in the society. Those different factors can be mainly divided into four different forms:

- Individual factor.
- Relationship factor.
- Community factor.
- Societal factor.

Man is not an individual. He is a social organism. God loves him only who serves other beings-child is exclusive one among them. One invisible factor, which always plays a vital role either to minimize the contribution of child abuse and at the sometime it increase rate of child abuse in the society. However there cannot be specific demarcation between those groups and how they work. They are complimentary and supplementary to each other sometime one particular factor may be predominant over the situation. They are interrelated and some time they are overlapping to each other.

Individual Factor

Individual factor deals with biological needs and variables with the personal history of a person that can influence an individual's susceptibility to child abuse. A factor in parents and caregivers increased risk of child abuse/neglect is also associated with the presence of certain factors in the parent or other family member. These include the parent or caregiver who:

- That, due to social disorganization family bonding is weaken as a result of which, it is difficult to establish new bonding with a newborn child as established earlier – as a result, for example, of a difficult pregnancy, birth complications, disappointment with the baby or gender bias etc.
- That, due to neglect of child, child became diseased child. It create a unbearable situation and adverse impact on family and on the economy policy of the family.
- That, due to various form of physical punishment as a means of discipline to the children, without analysing its outcome or result of it.
- That, due to loosening of self-control by the adult members, when they upset or angry.
- That, due to intoxication and use of drugs also, the ability and responsibility to take cares for the child is affected.
- That due to involvement of child in criminal activities, adversely affects the relationship between parent and child.
- That, due to social isolation of parent or caretaker usually exposes the child towards abuse.
- That due to poor parenting skills as a result of young age or lack of education to deal with situation.
- That, due to financial constraints inside the family.

There are certain other causes, which focus to the child, but it does not mean that the child is solely responsible for the abusive processes, which he/she faced. There is also some other circumstances compels to do this, it became more difficult situation for parents to deal with such situation these are as follows:

Unwanted baby or failed to fulfils the parent's expectations or wishes in terms, for instance, of its sex, appearance, temperament etc. Infant with high needs for example mentally or physically disabled child has a chronic illness, or who was born prematurely, cries constantly; physical features, such as facial abnormalities, that the parent has an aversion to and reacts to by withdrawing from the child shows symptoms of mental ill health.

Demonstrates personality or temperament traits that are perceived by the parent as problematic such as hyperactivity or impulsivity; multiple children from one pregnancy.

A sibling/sublings are possibly close in age but those who are demanding of parental attention; child that either exhibits or is exposed to dangerous behaviour problems, such as intimate partner violence, criminal behaviour, self-abusive behaviour, abuse towards animals, or persistent aggression with peers.

Relationship Factor

Human being is a social animal, on the one hand man is bound by blood kinship – his parents, his wife, his children and on the other, he is linked with every individual of society, apart from parents a social bondage established, that is called relation. Influences the level of an individual's close social contacts *i.e.,* for instance, with other family members in a family, they live together or as friends, that influence the individual's risk of both perpetrating and suffering for neglect or abusive process. The settings in which social relationships take place – such as neighbourhoods, workplaces and schools – and the particular characteristics of those settings that can contribute to child abuse. A sound family atmosphere both at the home and outside the home including good peer group and good schooling, motivate the child to develop positive attitude for his proper growth and development. The composition of families may vary greatly according to their own unique circumstances and to the norms of the local society. In many communities, the 'traditional' nuclear family of a married mother and father with children may not be the norm. Families may be lead by single mothers, single fathers, same-gender couples, siblings or elders.

Other factors for child abuse and neglect that may apply to relationships with family, friends, intimate partners and peers includes:

- Due to lack of parent – child attachment and failure to bond.
- Due to physical – developmental or mental health problems of a family member.
- Due to family breakdown – such as problems with a marriage or intimate relationship – that results in child or adult mental ill health, unhappiness, loneliness, tension or disputes over custody.
- Due to violence in the family, between parenting partners, between children or between parenting partners and children.
- Due to gender roles and roles in intimate relationships, including marriage, that are disrespectful of one or more persons in the household.
- Due to Isolation amongst the community.
- Due lack of a support network to assist with stressful or difficult situations in a relationship; Breakdown of support in child rearing from the extended family.
- Due to discrimination against the family because of ethnicity, nationality, religion, gender, age, sexual orientation, disability or lifestyle.
- Due to Involvement on the criminal activities.

Community Factor

The presence of several key factors and the situation in a community can precipitate abuse and events that may or may not occur otherwise. From those factors some situation widely spread in our state those are alcohol consumption, and the characteristics of the physical environment and firearms. A fourth important situational factor is the presence of gangs or organized armed groups within the community.

There is still some acceptance in the community for the use of physical force for the purposes of discipline and punishment of children. When held strongly by individual parents, these attitudes can support the physical and emotional abuse of children. This behaviour would not be tolerated between adults. Some adults engage in physical and sexual violence towards other adults and children. This violence may often stem from individual psychological problems, low self-esteem and a history of abuse and violence in their own childhood. Sex offenders hurt children because of a range of complex psychological and emotional problems for the lack of community understanding and support about the consequences.

Alcohol

Some children are not fortunate enough to have good parental care and sound family atmosphere. Consuming alcohol is a known factor in intimate partner violence, and this often directly affects children. Alcohol is also an important factor in violence against and by older children in community settings. In many societies, alcohol is common in social situations. Young people may use alcohol to bolster their self-confidence, and their aggression levels may increase and escalate to produce violent confrontations.

Environment

The nature of a community's physical fabric, its density of settlement and layout, and the availability of services and amenities supportive of family well-being, have an important bearing on social relationships within the community and on whether or not adults and children become prey to violence. Characteristics of community environments those are associated with an increased risk on child abuse. Those include:

- Tolerance of violence.
- Gender and social inequality in the community.
- Lack of or inadequate housing.
- Lack of services to support families and institutions and to meet specialised needs.

Among the most frequent community health concerns related to family housing are the inadequate supply of affordable housing for low-income people and the increasing spatial segregation of households by income, race, ethnicity, or social class into unsafe neighbourhoods. In its 2005 State of the World's Children Report, UNICEF reported that more than one out of every three children in the developing world lives in inadequate housing (approximately 640 million children). One in five does not have access to safe water (approximately 400 million children). While child homelessness is perhaps the most visible and dire violation of children's housing rights, all violations of housing rights, from forced eviction to inadequate housing conditions, have special ramifications for children. While forced evictions are universally detrimental to all their victims, they have special implications for children. Forced evictions are often accompanied by violence, particularly against women and children who are most likely to be at home when such a procedure is carried out. Evidence suggests that in response to the violence, panic and confusion so often characteristic of forced eviction, many children experience recurrent nightmares, anxiety and distrust. The impacts on family stability and the emotional well-being of children can be devastating, even when evictions are followed by immediate relocation. Children also have recounted increased incidents of violence within their own homes after a forced eviction had taken place.

Gangs

Gangs are an important factor in violence among and against children in many parts of the world. The gang fights and violent gang initiation practices among some of the poorest communities, often involving children living on the street, non-school goers as well as among the school students the gangs are formed and attract to become a member. However, their membership is accepted then the gangs are operating in and around schools can expose students and teachers to criminal activity and extreme violence. Research shows that, in many societies, physical and verbal aggression, including fighting, is considered a healthy and normal way for boys to prove their manhood and that explains, in part, why boys are more inclined to join gangs than girls and why boys' gangs enter into aggressive competition with other gangs. However, there are also gangs made up of girls and, like gangs of boys, they may also engage in violence. 132 Although gangs of boys on the streets are almost universally associated – in the public's mind – with violence, crime, and other forms of antisocial behaviour, it should be remembered that children – mostly but not exclusively boys – join gangs for a variety of reasons. In some cases, lack of nurturing and emotional support at home may prompt young teenagers to seek gang membership; in others, gang affiliation is the only means of achieving economic sufficiency for feeling safe.

Urbanisation

In this 21st century, the processes of urbanisation in the developing countries are rapidly in acceleration. Cities and towns are now home to around half of the worlds children. The process of relocation and its accompanying social changes, together with a lack of economic opportunity for those in the lowest educational, lowest skilled and lowest socio-economic groups, has helped to create circumstances favouring frustration and unrest, potentially leading to violence. Although urbanisation has historically been accompanied by lower rates of child mortality, increased access to education, and improvements across all social indicators, it also has negative aspects including poverty, inequality, changes in family structure and the breakdown of social networks – factors that all contribute to violence. The pace and irregular form of urbanisation has put under severe pressure the capacity of municipal authorities to provide services and amenities. Much of the housing in newly urbanised areas is cramped, flimsy, and insecure, while the surrounding environment does not offer many opportunities for children to play and interact safely with the world about them. Outdoor space in which they enter at an early age – is often contaminated by garbage and human waste. Due to Poverty, unemployment, migration in search of employment, attraction for urban life, industrialization are provided to be the potent reasons which make families incapable to provide all basic needs of children. There are various categories of children face many abuses, when they are out of home generally designated as street children, working children, deprived children, children in need of care and protection and juveniles in conflict with law.

Sexual Violence by Strangers in the Community

Someone known to the child, either from the family or within the family circle, more commonly perpetrates sexual violence against children but people outside these circles also perpetrate a significant number of sexual assaults on children in many countries. The Perpetrators can include a wide variety of people, some who may have planned the assault. A selection of available studies shows the range and seriousness of sexual violence inadequate policies and programmes within institutions that make the occurrence of child abuse more complex.

Societal Factor

Society influences the child abuse, the social norms generally encourages the harsh physical punishment to the children. There are an economic inequalities and in the absence of social welfare safety nets. There is already exists a substantial body of knowledge about the increase of more susceptibility to child abuse.

Child abuse may include:

- Social, economic, health and education policies that lead to poor living standards or to socio-economic inequality or instability.
- Social and cultural norms that promote or glorify violence towards others, including physical punishment – as depicted in the media, in popular music and in video games.
- Social and cultural norms that demand rigid gender roles for males and females; and diminish the status of the child in parent – child relationships; the existence of child pornography, child prostitution and child labour.
- Increase in mobility decrease homogeneous neighbourhood, a condition of anonymity was created and a child friendly environment was weakened.

Family Environment

Violence is likely to result from a combination of personal, familial, social, economic and cultural factors, and the interrelationship amongst these factors can be difficult to disentangle. Moreover, some children are exposed to several types of violence from multiple sources over many years. Environment inside the family contributes more about the conditions. As violence in the home is found in all social and economic spheres, studies from a range of different settings show that low parental education levels, lack of income, and household overcrowding increase the risk of physical and psychological violence against children. Physically violent parents are also more likely to be young, single and poor. These associations are likely to be related to stress caused by poverty, unemployment and social isolation. Children living in families with these factors are most at risk when there is inadequate social support and the family is not part of a strong social network. Lack of extended family support may exacerbate existing problems.

Stress and Social Isolation

The industrialised and developing countries study show that many of the personality and behavioural characteristics of violent parents related to poor social functioning and diminished capacity to cope with stress. Parents with poor impulse control, low self-esteem, mental health problems, and substance abuse (alcohol and drugs) are more likely to use physical violence against their children and/or to neglect them. Parents who use violence against their children may well have experienced violence as children. Since they spend more time at home, children in the early years – when they are most subject to influence by external factors and liable to be more overwhelmed by fear – are at particular risk of witnessing intimate partner violence. Such children may also learn powerful lessons about aggression in interpersonal relationships which they carry with them into their future.

Child development specialists suggest that hostile styles of behaviour, emotional regulation and the capacity for personal conflict resolution are shaped by parent – child and inter-parental relationships. However, not all children who grow up in violent homes suffer long-lasting consequences; given support, children have remarkable capacities for coping, and resilience in the face of violence.

Social Culture

The social culture constructs some Legal and policy framework in aid of our culture but the weak legal frameworks contribute both directly and indirectly to family violence against children. The laws of some countries still condone, either explicitly or implicitly as a result of interpretation, some level of violence against children, if it is inflicted by the child's own parents or guardians as a means of behavioural correction. In India, due to lack of legal protection against harmful traditional practices are child marriage, etc. Laws and policies relating to access to family planning services, alcohol availability, acceptable levels of environmental toxins, access to mental health and substance abuse treatment, and access to birth, death and marriage registration, have an indirect but substantial impact on the risk of child maltreatment in homes and families. Policies regarding education, child care, parental leave, health care, unemployment and social security that leave children and families without economic and social safety nets exacerbate family stress and social isolation and contribute to higher rates of violence against children. Membership in ethnic minority or indigenous groups: Children in ethnic minority groups are often at high risk of violence because of a confluence of other risk factors associated with the social exclusion of these groups. These include high rates of substance abuse and alcoholism, poverty, bad housing, and unemployment.

Family Isolation

Families, those who are socially isolated are sometimes not able to find people to support them if they start having problems with their children. Often families who are isolated have no extended family network and often feel left out of their community. Sometimes, families experience isolation because of the loss of a parent through death or separation. Some families experience isolation because they become homeless and have to live in temporary accommodation.

Domestic Violence

As such witnessing factor domestic violence is found inside home, the chaos and instability which is the result of an emotional abuse to a child. Frequently domestic violence will escalate to physical violence against the child. Parenting can be a very time intensive, difficult job. Parents caring for children without support from family, friends or the community can be under a lot of stress. Teen parents often struggle with the maturity and patience needed to be a parent. Caring for a child with a disability, special needs or difficult behaviours is also a challenge. Caregivers who are under financial or relationship stress are at risk as well. Alcohol and drug abuse lead to serious lapses in judgment. They can interfere with impulse control making emotional and physical abuse more likely. Due to impairment caused by being intoxicated, alcohol and drug abuse frequently lead to child neglect. The infants are vulnerable to as a result of omission and neglect. Infants are most vulnerable in the time immediately after birth; they remain extremely vulnerable, but become decreasingly so, throughout their first year and early childhood (0 to 4 years). A child's sex may also be a factor which raises his or her risk of victimisation. Although sexual violence is frequently directed against boys, girls are more likely to suffer such abuse. Daughters are more likely to be severely neglected in societies where son preference is pronounced, while in some societies sons are more likely to experience severe violence than daughters.

Child with Disability

Children with disabilities are at heightened risk of violence for a variety of reasons, ranging from deeply ingrained cultural prejudices to the higher emotional, physical, economic, and social demands that a child's disability can place on his or her family. Children with physical, sensory, intellectual or mental health disabilities endure almost double the number of violent incidents compared to their non-disabled peers. Children with chronic illness or serious behavioural problems may be at increased risk of neglect.

Environmental Risk Factors

Where the environment is itself full of risk, children who work in open spaces are constantly exposed to violence. In some places, work in the service industries such as restaurants and shops may expose young workers to armed robbery or customer aggression. When working children feel constantly threatened by violence in the environment, they may also learn violent behaviours themselves or become behaviourally disturbed, exhibiting sexual or personal aggression. Work on the street or in transport, shops, bars or hotels based in shanty-town areas known for their violence presents special risks to the children involved. Illicit activities such as trade in illegal goods are by their nature conducted in high-risk areas where criminal enterprises are part of the environment.

School and Institutional Care Environment

Next to family child spend more time in preschool, school, vocational institution, institution for children care either run by the government or non-government organization, where they learn behaviour and approach to world at a large. Here discipline is the vital question to make the young men into discipline civilized citizen, many methodology are adopted where punishment play a vital role. Many people believe that only punishment makes adolescent and child into a discipline life today's punishment is a lesson to the child and he or she cannot repeated it further. It is obvious that child involve in school violence directly or indirectly as a victim. Whether perpetrated by adults or children, almost all violence in schools reflects a 'hidden curriculum' that promotes gender inequality and stereotyping. For example, boys taunt each other about their lack of masculinity and harass girls with verbal and physical gestures that are sexual in nature. Corporal punishment of boys is more frequent and harsh than corporal punishment of girls. Sexual aggression by male teachers and boys is often dismissed as 'just boys being boys', while girls are blamed for 'asking for it'. The implicit messages are that males should be tough, generally and sexually assertive and ready for life in a rough-and-tumble world but females should be passive, sheltered, and unassertive, particularly sexually. These stereotypes often make schools unsafe and uncomfortable for girls, and in some part of country girls attending school less than boys.

In both institutional care unit and schools, corporal punishment and other forms of cruel or degrading punishment have been widely favoured methods of 'discipline' perceived as 'taming' the unruly child, training the presumptuous child to take his or her 'proper place' in the social order, and hardening the unseasoned child to the difficult, brutal and abrasive world. Before twentieth century beating, humiliation and isolation were routinely used as methods of teaching and discipline.

Child Mal-Adjustment

A child's mal-adjustment can be defined as the child's capacity "to cope successfully with everyday challenges including life transitions, times of cumulative stress and significant adversity or risk. Typically, resilient children are recognised by their high self-esteem, internal locus of control, optimism and clear aspirations, achievement and goal-orientation, reflection and problem-solving capacity, healthy communication patterns, and the capacity to seek out mentoring adult relationships.

Schools can play a critical role in building children's adjustment in school environment and feelings of well-being with other creature in the earth, which have also been linked to the reduced likelihood of being victimized. Adults and peers in children's families and communities begin building, or failing to build, children's resilience from birth. Good parenting in stable family units is critical. The power of early parent – child bonds established within warm and supportive family relationships, along with high levels of parental care during early childhood, are important in building resilience.

But even when families or communities fail, schools can compensate, especially when they provide strong support from the early years. Schools can also provide bridges between children and their families and communities, helping families and communities to understand how they affect children and to acquire the skills to become more supportive. In addition, schools can promote the development of strong peer group and social bonds to build resilience, as well as build empathy, conflict management skills and critical thinking.

While support from their families and peers is critical to making children less vulnerable to violence in schools, an increasing body of research confirms that the systematic attention to the behaviour of the school heads, teachers and other school staff is also critical. If they engage in abusive behaviour and show disrespect for the rights, comfort and safety of others, then children's will.

There is evidence to suggest that fierce peer competition, gender-based violence and gang violence within schools are all, to some extent, related to the stresses that go with modernization and industrialization. These phenomena are all more commonly reported from the urban areas of industrialized or rapidly industrializing countries than from rural areas of less developed areas.

Low Priority

Low priority is found in Indian school because there is so many constrain of other factor are responsible. There is private and government runs school and institutional care unit for children. Low level of funding, lack of skilled professional, and lack of attitude for children growth is the additional factors for low priority. Few institutions set up by Governments under human rights obligations for those children who have been orphaned, abandoned, those living with disabilities, or in conflict with the law. Those children needing care and protection outside the family due to the focus of policy but it fail to attend his goal because of its conditions those are in residential place for children and juvenile detention centres' are poor, with inadequate facility like nutrition, hygiene and health care.

Inadequate Staffing

Unqualified and poorly remunerated staffs are widely recognised as a key factor linked to violence within institutions. Low pay and status frequently result in poorly motivated employees and rapid staff turnover, and under-staffing is a serious problem. For example, *Sikhya Shayaka* are very ill-paid and there is no regular teacher in school and they perform as a teacher in the classroom and it all so documented that staffing ratios in institutions for children is a ratio one teacher for hundred children. It is further noted that children with disabilities the staffing ratios in institutions also very high as one hundred children for each staff. Under such conditions, children are often left unattended for long periods, and overnight entire wards are unattended or padlocked, with only a skeleton night shift.

Physical and emotional abuses in such instances are very common and few staffs in care institutions receive any special training in child development or rights, or information about issues of violence. In institutions for children with disabilities, inadequately trained staff can be quick to lash out at the children. Overwhelmed staff may resort to violent measures to maintain discipline, particularly when supervision is lacking. Staff 'burnout' results in increasingly negative attitudes towards children and in patterns of physical and impulsive responses to confrontation.

Individuals with histories of violence against children, including sexual abuse and exploitation superficially and prosecutions are extremely rare. Those in a position to take action may be complicit in the abuse, reluctant to discipline or prosecute a colleague, or fearful of negative publicity or loss of financial support. They may respond by blocking access to the institutions; punishing or threatening to dismiss workers if they speak out. The failure to hold perpetrators accountable only ensures that violence continues. Perpetrators go on to abuse other may seek out jobs that allow them easy access to children. Rigorous background checks on personnel are still rare, allowing an employee who has been dismissed from one institution to be hired by another and to continue a pattern of abuse.

Failure to supervise staff properly is also a serious problem and ineffective management and minimal contact by managers with staff as significant features common to the child abuse.

Lack of Monitoring in Institutional Care

Residential care and detention facilities are mixing which make different levels of vulnerability, and many facilities fail to segregate vulnerable children from dangerous inmates. Children who are vulnerable to violence because of age, size, sex or other characteristics are often housed together with older children with a history of violent behaviour. It is report that children under the age of seven may be placed in the same institution as child offenders over the age where children in need of care and protection are often housed with children charged with offences, investigation committee found that gangs of older children usually physically, emotionally and sexually abuse on young children. In many places children in detention are held with adult offenders, greatly increasing their risk of violence. Often unregulated and closed to outside scrutiny, especially those run by private agencies, faith-based organizations, and NGOs, or that are situated in isolated areas. In such circumstances, violence may continue for years until an extreme incident brings it to light. Moreover, individuals responsible for violence against children in care and justice systems are rarely held accountable for their actions. If cases are reported, they often are only investigated, and no proper action taken.

Violence by Staff

Although the State is responsible for protecting children from violence irrespective of who is providing their care, staff violence has been documented in institutions including those run by the State, NGO or by faith-based organizations, and by private entrepreneurs or enterprises. The forms of violence can be horrific. Physical, sexual and psychological violence by staff is common in residential facility school and correctional home. Such violence can include verbal abuse, beatings, excessive restraints, rape, sexual assault or harassment. Some time it comes in the form of disciplinary action In some statute there are detailed regulations specifying how punishment is to be administered, including the implement to be used.

Specific Abuse to Girl Child

In many places of Odisha and other part of India, there are local schools for young children are far distance from they are staying. Many parents willing not to send their children to the far distance place for studying and at the same time some people have home for boarding schools, or to live with relatives for the higher primary grades and secondary school. This is often the case in regions where populations are scattered through rural areas, perhaps in mountains or other hard-to access locations. Parents fear that their girls may be assaulted on the way there or back, on the road, or in crowded buses.

In some societies with low levels of girls' education, the seclusion of girls at home after puberty is still common, and the same is true of early marriage. Even where seclusion is not practiced, research shows that parents fear for their girls' sexual safety in school. A Human Rights Watch study on gender-based violence in schools found alarming levels of sexual violence against schoolgirls, and a frightening degree of tolerance and collusion by teachers. Such situation build a pressure group on child leave school and accept crude traditional form of family life and when those girls have its own child started same type of abuse to her children.

Abuse to Disable Children in Course of their Treatment

Violence against children in care and justice systems is legitimised by long-held attitudes and behaviours, and failures in both law and its implementation. At the time when the establishment of care institutions for children in disadvantaged and marginal groups was a preferred social policy, corporal punishment was almost universally endorsed for the discipline and control of unruly children. This effectively meant that institutionalised children were exposed to a brutal regime and to frequent violence. In all regions, by omission or commission, this situation still prevails in India.

A further example of State-authorised violence is the practice of performing medical interventions to limit reproductive functions – for example, giving hysterectomies to young girls with intellectual impairments or mental health concerns. In some places it is found that young girls at the age of seven or eight get mutation, but there is no medical justification for such operations. However, several reasons have been given for its justification, that the operation will prevent the girls from menstruating, thus avoiding demands that would otherwise be placed on caregivers; and that it will ensure that the young girl will not become pregnant. Such concerns reflect the problems of understaffed institutions and the lack of sexual and reproductive health education and services for girls with disabilities, as well as the lack of adequate protection against the assumed risk of rape for young women both in institutions and the community. In residential institutions for children with disabilities (including brain injuries, developmental disabilities, and psychiatric disabilities), children may be subjected to violence as part of their purported 'treatment.' For example, the SIBIS (Self Injurious Behaviour-Inhibiting System) device is a commercially available remote-controlled electric shock device marketed almost exclusively for administering shocks to children with disabilities. One facility in the United States devised its own 'substantially stronger' device when it found that electrical shocks from the SIBIS device 'lost much of (their) effectiveness' over a period of a few months.

Another example is in the psychiatric institutions, young children were subjected to electroconvulsive or 'shock' treatment (ECT) without the use of muscle relaxants or anaesthesia. Such treatment is extremely painful, frightening and dangerous. Electric shocks are also used as an 'aversive treatment' to control children's behaviour in some institutions. Drugs may also be used not for medical treatment, but coping with shortage of staff and to control children's behaviour not to make 'compliant'. This may have other implications when children with disabilities are heavily medicated by staff in institutions and hospitals they are unable to defend themselves from physical violence or sexual assault.

Neglecting

Wherever children are living, including when they are in the custody of the State, Governments are required to ensure that basic needs are met. However, conditions in many residential institutions are often so poor that they put the health and lives of children at risk. Institutions are often overcrowded, unsanitary, and lacking in both staff and resources, leading to increased mortality rates among these children compared to their peers in family environments.

In rehabilitation centres for children with mental disabilities bedridden children emaciated from starvation and dehydration have been found. Bottles of food were provided by staff, but children who were unable to pick up the bottles due to their disability got no nourishment. In many facilities for children with disabilities, the children have no access to education, recreation, rehabilitation or other programmes. They are often left in their beds or cribs for long periods without human contact or stimulation. Such deprivation often leads to severe negative physical, mental and psychological damage and in many instances to death.

Children in residential care are vulnerable to violence from their peers, particularly when conditions and staff supervision are poor. Lack of privacy and respect for cultural identity, frustration, overcrowding, and a failure to separate particularly vulnerable children from older, more aggressive children often lead to peer-on-peer violence. Staff may sanction or encourage peer abuse amongst children – either to maintain control or simply for amusement.

Abuse in Work Environment

Children are exposed to violence in the workplace is common but most difficult to address and to find out why children are in work place and how they are exploited. According to international instruments and national laws children under a certain age (below 14) should not be in the workplace. Violence is a neglected aspect of debates on child labour; there are little data available, especially for child workers in the informal economy where the majority are to be found. Violence towards working children has only remained 'invisible' because the direct question is rarely posed.

The most obvious response to violence against children in the workplace is to remove them from it. However, it is important to recognise that for many children this is not an easy option. Programmers to remove children from violent workplaces have to ensure that the reasons they are there – economic, social and cultural – are simultaneously addressed, or they will simply return to them. Unless programmed engage with child workers and their families and seek to change attitudes, expectations and prospects, they are not likely to remove children permanently from an exploitative working life.

The International Labour Organization has developed a conceptual framework for analysing violence at work among the general worker population, viewing it as function of four interrelated factors:

- Characteristics of the child victims.
- Characteristics of the perpetrators.

- The work environment.
- Risks factor in the place of work.

Though not developed with child workers in mind, this framework is helpful in capturing a number of interactive features, including individual and social risk factors, the context in which certain types of work are performed, and individual and social outcomes, and workplace costs.

Characteristics of Victim and Perpetrators

Children are more vulnerable to violence than adult workers due to their age, small size, mental immaturity, and state of dependence. The distance of the employer in terms of space, social and ethnic affiliation from the child's background affects whether he or she feels responsibility for the young worker's well-being. In addition to this social, ethnical and traditional practices make children into more vulnerable, boys are more expose to physical violence and girls are more vulnerable to sexual violence where children with disabilities are at elevated risk of violence. Children are also less likely than adults to physically resist violence or make complaints, making them easy targets. Young workers, whether they have attained the legal working age or not, are usually at the bottom of the workplace hierarchy. Disability may also play a part in violence against working children. In many parts of the world, for example, there are frequent reports of children with visible disabilities being sent out to earn a living as beggars, often suffering physical violence if they do not earn enough during their 'working day'. Such practices are not only painful, exploitative and humiliating for the children, but frequently contribute to worsening their disabilities and undermining their health.

The power relationship of employer over worker exacerbates risk; this power is absolute since the job is in the boss's hands. Available information on recorded cases of workplace violence against children implies that most consists of violence inflicted by employers, since the majority of children work informally for 'employers', a term that includes anyone who has a controlling relationship over a working child. Perpetrators also include foremen, co-workers, customers, police, and criminal gangs. Vulnerability is enhanced where the working situation is isolated or illegal; children in the sex trade often fall under the control of pimps or brothel owners.

Risks related to the workplace itself vary according to whether the working activity takes place in an organized setting, such as a factory or an informal setting, such as a backroom enterprise; whether the workplace has special characteristics of remoteness or danger, such as: mines, fishing, quarrying, and some types of agriculture; whether it consists of a closed environment such as a household; or whether it is part of an illegal activity (sexual exploitation or drug dealing). The most extreme examples of workplace violence against children occur within the worst forms of child labour.

Children in unsafe working environments are at constant risk of violence. Such environments include glass factories, mining, and plantation agriculture, especially where health and safety regulations are not existent. Severe injuries can result from dangerous machinery, guns, accidents, toxic fumes and explosions. All such ill-effects affect young and growing bodies and minds more than those of adults. Reports from a range of countries of systemic workplace abuse against children include for example: inhumane conditions in the cotton industry and unsafe use of pesticides around agricultural workers, including children.

3 International and National - Perspective

There has been an enormous development and significance at the horizon of International Law and the International community is closely involved in achieving higher standards. Human Rights are fundamental entitlements that all persons enjoy as protection against state-conduct prohibited by International Law or custom, when the International and National Rights embark a remarkable caption subject regarding rights of a human being. Man is born with Human Rights and it is birthright which is inalienable Right; then why do mankind and children's are suffering from lot of problems such as 'child abuse' in the *rem*. In India, the problem of child abuse has steadily assuming a serious proposition in the wake of Industrialization, urbanisation, socio-cultural transformation, eroded value system, disintegration of families, wide spread poverty and inequalities and lastly rapid growth of population. Physical and Mental hardships and exploitation of minors especially in the metropolis also contributed substantially to this serious problem. It enlightened the present form of rights in so far as it relates to child abuse. Kofi Annan the then secretary general of the United Nations pointed out in his views "To look into some aspects of the future, we do not need projections by super computers. Much of the next millennium can be seen in how we care for our children today. "Tomorrow's world may be influenced by science and technology, but more than anything, it is already taking shape in the bodies and minds of our children" it explicitly specifies the duty of mankind in discharging their responsibility towards the promotion and protection of the rights of the children in their future well-being. On going through in the History of International Jurisprudence, one can certainly arrive at the conclusion that efforts were made to inculcate the morale standards in the matter of child at the International level, as Children are not the property to their parents but products of the States, and they are people in the making; being subject of civil society. The family and the state have moral, ethical and legal obligations to recognise the rights of the children on par with that of individuals of society at all levels without any discrimination. In spite of the onerous responsibility which lies on the shoulders of the national and international community, it took a long time for the world to recognise the human rights of the children. With the adoption of the Declaration of the Rights of the child by the League of Nations in 1924, the modern civilized world for the first time recognised explicitly that children too have rights. After the adoption of the Declaration, it took a long time to convert the declaration into a legal instrument, in spite of various efforts taken by the United Nation's, the continuous sustainable efforts of UN have finally culminated the adoption of Convention on the Rights of the Child. On 20th November, 1989. That came into force in less than a year in September 1990. The Universal Declaration of Human Rights as a common standard of achievement for all people and all nations says that every individual and every organ of society shall strived educating and teaching people to promote these rights and freedoms.

The International Federation of the Red Cross and Red Crescent Societies in the World Disaster Report, 2001 states that, on an average, 242 million people were affected by natural disaster or armed conflict, each year, 'between' 1991 to 2000.

Of this number, at least 76.5 million were children under the age of 15 and the vast majority *i.e.* 75 million lived in developing countries. The data of human and economic loss due to disasters in this current decade is much more alarming than this particularly in Asian region. However, there is little global data on the breakdown of affected populations by age, though media reports show that children form one of the largest segments of populations affected by the recent few horrifying natural and man-made disasters. Research studies and good practices on how to address children's capacities and vulnerabilities in times of disaster are very few in number, when compared to the number of children affected. Many examples of disaster reports (Gujarat earthquake and Bangladesh flood, SPHERE Project, etc.,) hardly mention on these issues of children in their reports, although the social dimension of vulnerability assessment has been emphasising on the vulnerability of children along with women. Disaster literature confines them to three areas: *(i)* they are part of studies on women, *(ii)* they are treated as the cohorts of psychiatric or psychological studies, and *(iii)* they become 'icons' of suffering and sign of perilous plight (Marten, 2001). In the eventuality of the recent tsunami, many media reports stated about the danger of sexual abuse and exploitation of children in many affected countries. Any disaster planning and measure need to look at children as a separate category of victims in any disaster as they represent more than 50 per cent of the populations of many countries in developing world, thus represent a sizeable proportion of individuals affected by all types of disasters.

In order to obtain a global estimate of the numbers of economically active children, one would need reliable and comparable statistics for every country. Child labour is a complex problem, whose roots are deeply embedded in cultural, social, economic structures and traditions. Child pornography as well as an unknown fraction of pornography is a serious threat to National and International levels. In recent years there have been increased international agreements to outlaw child pornography but the means of communication development with recent practice in which people use cell phone messaging to send nude or semi nude images of themselves to others (such as friends or dating partners). These may be passed along to others or be posted on the internet. Due to sex testing by minors, some teenagers have been charged with possessing and/or distributing child pornography resulting in unintended look like photographs may also be considered by many to be child pornography. Trafficking in persons especially women and children has become an important issue transcending borders, affecting countries all over the world. An estimated 2, 25,000 victims are trafficked from South East Asia annually according to the US Department of States. Sri Lanka and India are the favoured destinations of sex tourists from other parts of the world. As a pull factor, information technology, particularly Internet, has been increasingly used to market women and children for the purposes of pornography, prostitution and matrimony. Tourism industry has grown worldwide and especially in developing countries, as a part and parcel of globalisation. Tourists come to the developing countries from different parts of the world for easy and cheap sexual gratification especially with children. The HIV/AIDS pandemic are having a devastating effect on children. This includes the 13 million children orphaned by AIDS, the nearly 600,000 infants infected every year through mother-to-child transmission and the millions of HIV-positive young people are living with this stigma. In number of other areas, some of them sensitive, the convention goes beyond existing legal standards and practices. It is pity to limelight here that, in the year 2008 a review of child pornography laws with in 187 countries by the International Centre for Missing and Exploited Children (ICMEC) shows that 93 country have no laws that specifically address child pornography, rest of that 94 that do but 36 do not criminalize the possession of child pornography. The conflation of trafficking with migration has brought forth many undesirable consequences. Trafficking is essentially a labour problem for it is done for placing of holding a person, where most of these people work without pay or on a low pay in bad conditions of work, with poor health and safety measures. Most of them end up being in debt bondage. Therefore, trafficking as labour problem brings to light many gross violations of labour rights of trafficked persons. Child labour as understood, keeping this in view, on 20th November 1989, the international community extended the mantle of human rights protection to children when it adopted the United Nations Convention on the Rights of the Child. This is the first international legal instrument, which guarantees human rights for children; the Convention, which accept the Convention legally accountable for their actions towards children. The guiding spirit of the convention is the 'best interest of the child' positive and forward-looking in its approach, the Convention calls on states, which ratify it to create the conditions in which children may take an active and creative part in the social and political life of their countries. Human rights are inalienable rights, which start at the time of birth; children are equally entitled to human rights in the same way as adult do. In India, it is fundamental that it must be outlawed without compromise. To reaffirm faith in various International conventions, a committee of ten experts which will generate a permanent dialogue involving all parties concerned with the promotions of children's rights State parties will submit reports to the Committee on how they are carrying out the Convention and on difficulties they face in doing so.

India is a signatory to a number of international instruments and declarations pertaining to the rights of children for protection, security and dignity. In discharging the constitutional obligations India adopted a National Policy of Children in 1974 and constituted a National Children's Welfare Board. Apart from the Board, it has constituted, a National Human Rights Commission in 1993 through the Human Rights Act in order to augment the human rights of all sections of the Indian polity including that of children. At this juncture in order to halt the exploitation of children, the Commission has taken substantial interest in the promotion and protection of the rights since in its inception. It has established a Human Rights Committee (here in after referred as Committee), which makes recommendations on cases related to violations of human rights on the basis of a quasi-judicial determination. The United Nations Convention on the Rights of the Child (UNCRC) in 1992, reaffirming its earlier acceptance of the 1959 UN Declaration on the Rights of the Child, and it fully committed in implementation of all provisions of the UN CRC. In 2005, the Government of India accepted the two Optional Protocols to the UN CRC, addressing the involvement of children in armed conflict and the sale of children, child prostitution and child pornography. India is strengthening its national policy and measures to protect children from these dangerous forms of violence and exploitation. India is also a part to the International Conventions on Civil and Political Rights, and on Economic, Social and Cultural Rights which apply to the human rights of children as much as adults. A convention is an agreement between countries to obey the same law. When the government of a country ratifies a convention that means it agrees to obey the law written down in that convention.

Three important International Instruments for the protection of Child Rights in India are:

1. The (UN) Convention on the Rights of the Child (CRC) adopted by the General Assembly of the United Nation in 1989. Is the widely accepted UN instrument ratified by most of the developed as well as developing countries of the World including 'India' The Convention prescribes standards to be adhered to by all State parties in securing the best interest of the child and outlines the fundamental rights of children, including the right to be protected from economic exploitation and harmful work, from all forms of sexual exploitation and abuse and from physical or mental violence, as well as ensuring that children will not be separated from their families against their will.

2. Reaffirming that children's rights require special protection and call for continuous improvement of the situation of children all over the world, as well as for their development and education in conditions of peace and security.
3. Profoundly concerned that the situation of children in many parts of the world remains critical as a result of inadequate social conditions, natural disasters, armed conflicts, exploitation, illiteracy, hunger and disability, and convinced that urgent and effective national and international action is called for into the important role of the United Nations Children's Fund and of that of the United Nations in promoting the well-being of children and their development.

As outlined that an international convention on the rights of the child, as a standard-setting accomplishment of the United Nations in the field of human rights, would make a positive contribution to protecting children's rights and ensuring their well-being.

The year 1989 is marked as the thirteenth anniversary of the Declaration of the Rights of the Child and the tenth anniversary of the International Year of the Child. The Convention has been ratified by most of the developed as well as developing countries, including India, which ratified the Convention in 1992. The four major Articles pertaining to child abuse and neglect in the Convention are: Article 3: Protect the best interests of children; Article 19: Protect children from all forms of physical or mental violence, injury or abuse, neglect or negligent treatment, mal-treatment or exploitation, including sexual abuse while in the care of parents, legal guardians or any other person in whose care they are; Article 34: Undertake to protect children from all forms of sexual exploitation and sexual abuse; Article 35: Take all appropriate national, bilateral and multi-lateral measures to prevent the abduction of, sale of or traffic in children for any purpose or in any form.

The rising demand for child sex workers has spawned a vicious child trafficking industry. Tourism is regarded as an industry because it the prime source of foreign exchange and panacea to all the economic ills of a developing country. Tourism has been seen in developing countries as an opportunity for rapid economic development, bringing in much needed foreign exchange. The international tourism aims at supporting tourism to contribute on the economic development, international understanding, and promotion of peace, wealth and maintenance of human rights and freedom for all human beings without discrimination of race, sex, language, and religion. The phenomenon started in a small scale but mushroomed in several third world countries in a wide scale as a result of rapid industrialization and urbanisation after the Second World War .The organized sexual exploitation of children is a worldwide phenomenon, and one that increasingly appears to be taking on an international dimension, Child pornography, often involving the circulation of material produced in developing countries, the trafficking of children across national borders for exploitation, the movement of sexual exploitation of female domestic workers and 'child brides' are all features of this transnational exploitation, each of which essentially involves the movement of the child or pornographic material to the consumer.

The World Tourism Organization (WTO), adopted its first resolution on – as it was then called – the prevention of 'organized sex tourism' in which it denounced and condemned child sex tourism", considering it a violation of article 34 of the Convention on the Rights of the Child (CRC) and requiring strict legal action by tourist sending and receiving countries. State parties undertake to protect the child from all forms of sexual exploitation and sexual abuse. For these purposes, states parties shall in particular take all appropriate national, bilateral and multilateral measures to prevent:

(a) The inducement of coercion of child to engage in unlawful sexual activity.

(b) The exploitative use of children in prostitution or other unlawful sexual practices.

(c) The exploitative use of children in pornographic performances and materials.

Many international tourism organizations have passed resolutions and have declared their willingness to cooperate with the authorities on countering child sex abuse at all levels, while the above resolution remains on paper, over one million children in Asia alone are victims of tourism industry. One thing is certain, that the menace of child sexual abuse is now very much a widespread phenomenon in the Asian region as a whole. The above description makes it clear that so far as the sexual exploitation of children by tourists is concerned, Asian scenario is frightening and alarming and therefore, needs immediate preventive measures to stem the growth of this horrendous evil.

International Perspective

The globalisation of legitimate economic activities has been closely matched by the corresponding globalisation of organized crime. The same developments in area such as transportation and communication technologies, which have created enormous opportunities for human communication and economic development, have also created significant opportunities for organized crimes with in a form of child abuse and neglect. These following outlines lights the dark side of the scene. On 11th October, 2006 the United Nations (UN) released the first UN secretary general study on violence against children that address violence against children within family, schools, alternative care institutions and detention facilities, places where children work, and communities. The study took years to complete, and was supported by the United Nations children's Fund (UNICEF), the World Health Organization (WHO) and the office of the High Commissioner on Human Rights (OHCHR). As per the study it is first in two important ways:

1. "First comprehensive, global study conducted by the United Nations on all forms of violence against children".
2. "First global study to engage directly and consistently with children. Children have participated in all regional consultations held in connection with the study, eloquently describing both the violence they experience and their proposals for ending it" and the aforesaid report over view the following statistics.

- The World Health Organization estimates that 40 million children below the age of 15 suffer from abuse and neglect, and require health and social care.
- Up to 80 to 98 per cent of children suffer physical punishment in their homes, with a third or more experiencing severe physical punishment resulting from the use of implements.
- A survey in Egypt showed 37 per cent of children reporting being beaten by their parents, and 26 per cent reporting injuries.
- A (1995) survey in the US showed that 5 per cent of parents admitted disciplining their children through hitting the child with an object, kicking the child, beating the child, and threatening the child with a knife or gun.
- As per the estimate of 2000, those 1.8 million children were forced into prostitution and pornography, and 1.2 million were victims of trafficking.
- Almost 53,000 children died worldwide in 2002 as a result of homicide.
- As per the estimation 150 million girls and 73 million boys under age *i.e.* 18 had experienced forced sexual intercourse or other forms of sexual violence. In sub-Saharan Africa, Egypt and the Sudan, 3 million girls and women are subjected to genital mutilation/cutting every year.
- Recent South African Police statistics show 21,000 cases of child rape or assault reported against children as young as nine months old.
- In 2004, 218 million children were involved in child labour, of which 126 million were in hazardous work.

The UN Secretary General's Study on Violence against Children is an outcome of the gross violation of children's rights. It is a joint initiative, directly supported by the Office of the High Commissioner on Human Rights, UNICEF and WHO. The study is likely to provide an in-depth global picture of violence against children. Transnational organized crime poses a major challenge for legislators, prosecutors and law enforcement officials, who are facing an increase in the range of offences committed and volume of cases reported. The existing infrastructure of international co-operation is no longer adequate to respond to these challenges. The high cost and complexity of conducting multi-national investigations and prosecution exacerbates this situation. In recent years there have been increased international agreements to outlaw child pornography. The council of Europe's cyber crime Convention, the United Nations Optional Protocol on the Rights of the child, and the EU Framework Decisions that became active in, 2006. In order to address the complex dimensions of the problem and to take into account the full cycle from the roots and causes to their impacts and consequences at all the individual and societal level, an integrated and holistic approach needs to be evolved.

National Perspective

Today's children will be the leaders of tomorrow who will hold the countries banner high and maintain the prestige of Nation. If a child goes wrong for want of proper attention, training and guidance, it will indeed be a deficiency of the society and of the government of the day. A problem child is indeed a negative factor. Every society must, therefore, devote full attention to ensure that children are properly cared for and brought up in a proper atmosphere where they could receive adequate training, education and guidance in order that they may be able to have their rightful place in the society when they grow up. State parties are also to endeavour to undertake measures including information campaigns and social and economic activities to prevent child abuses. So in the national level also to adopt or strengthen legislative or other measures, such as educational, social or cultural measures, including bilateral and multilateral co-operation to discourage the demand that fosters all forms of exploitation of persons especially women and children, that leads to child abuse.

- The situation of children in India is deplorable. Almost 100 million children in India are out of school, despite the proactive stand by the government and the successful implementation of the Education for All programmes. Nearly 35 million children are homeless, according to an estimate, although there are homes for just about 36,000 children.
- Studies across India show child abuse to be prevalent in a rampant form. More than four lakh children in India are reported to be victims of commercial sexual exploitation. In Delhi alone, nearly four to five lakh children live on the streets, 53 per cent of young children suffer from malnutrition and 33 per cent of the 6-14 age groups are deprived of schooling.
- Averages of 44,476 children are reported missing in India every year, out of which 11,008 children continue to remain untraced. Most of these children end up in brothels or being abused by tourists.
- The extent of abuse inflicted on children gets reflected from the crime records data. The total crime against children showed a rising trend from 1999 to 2001, as 4,957 cases were registered in 1999 as against 6,087 cases in 2001. However, in the year 2002, such cases went down to 5,972. The total figure for crime against children for the year 2003 (2,084) is not comparable with the figures of the previous year as the figures of child rape are not included for the year 2003. Data on child rape are not collected on a monthly basis.
- Cases of infanticide (134) have increased by 16.5 per cent in 2003 compared to 115 in 2002. Maharashtra reported the highest cases of infanticide (30), which accounted for 22.4 per cent of the total infanticide cases in 2003.
- Cases of female foeticide have decreased by 38.1 per cent during 2003 (52) compared to 84 in 2002. Rajasthan reported the highest number of cases of foeticide (11), which alone accounted for 21.2 per cent of the total cases of foeticide in 2003.

- Incidence of kidnapping and abduction of children was around 700 in 1999 and 2000, which suddenly rose to 2,845 and 2,322 in 2001 and 2002 respectively and again went down to 765 in 2003. The highest number of cases of kidnapping and abduction of children was reported from Maharashtra and Gujarat.
- Cases of procreation of minor girls increased by 37.9 per cent in 2003 (171) compared to 124 in 2002. The highest number of 47 cases was reported from Bihar.
- Although incidence of child rape, one of the worst forms of sexual abuse, has declined between the periods 1999 and 2002, from 3153 cases to 2532, the unofficial number may have been higher since many cases may have not been reported. So is the case with kidnapping and abduction.

A comprehensive understanding of the phenomenon of child abuse is developed with a view to formulating appropriate policies and programmes in order to effectively curb and control the problem of child abuse in India. Unfortunate to note that, the child abuse cases, in the given sense, are generally not reported due to the fact that such an offence does not figure under any law (except the Goa Children's Act-2003), or due to the absence or inadequacy of legal provisions. It may also be on account of several cultural, socio-economic and psychological reasons. It becomes imperative to undertake a national level study on child abuse, since very few studies have been conducted in this extremely critical area. Child abuse, unfortunately, has not been viewed as a separate offence or group of offences, or state of body and mind, causing physical and emotional damage to the child. It is, at best, viewed in the context of child labour, child prostitution and child trafficking, for which legal provisions have been made. Forms and dynamics of child abuse have undergone major changes in recent decades, adding multifaceted dimensions, complexities and challenges. Most of the beaches are being thrown open to tourism. Special tourism areas are being demarcated in the most environmentally sensitive region, the coastal region of India. The problem of child abuse and the web of its human rights violation embrace some of the most critical aspects of the worst forms of child exploitation and abuse on the international human rights agenda: The 'rights of children', is one area on which the National Human Rights Commission (NHRC) has tried to focus continuously ever since it was constituted in October 1993. It observed from the very beginning that despite there being major provisions in the Constitution of India for survival, development and protection of children as well as laws to safeguard their interests including the fact that the Government of India had ratified the CRC, children all over the country, especially those belonging to weaker sections of the society, were found to be vulnerable and their dignity and human rights were often trampled. Though, the initial few months of the Commission were spent on making an overall assessment about the range of issues that affected children, but once this task was completed, the Commission concentrated its attention on preventing and eradicating the problems of child labour, child marriage, child trafficking and prostitution, child sexual violence, female foeticide and infanticide, child rape, HIV/AIDS in children and the problem of juveniles. In the year 2005 there has been implementation of national policies and strategies to build and strengthen governmental, family and community capacities to provide supportive environment for orphans and girls and boys infected and affected by HIV/AIDS, all forms of abuse, violence, exploitation, discrimination, trafficking and loss of inheritance. But another critical human and economic problem is that of child labour, poor parents seek to augment their meagre income through employment of their children. It is also of financial advantage to employers. A total prohibition on any form of child suffering may not be socially feasible in the prevailing socio-economic environment. Subject among other covered are many, many interdisciplinary international covenants and declaration are as follows:

Role of Covenants and Declarations

It will be of great significance to mention here that the role of the state is particularly critical in sustaining the delivery of basic social services compromising basic education, primary health care including nutrition programmed and food subsidies for the poor and low cost water and the sanitation services. It is now well established that investments in basic social services provide a sound foundation for sustainable and equitable human development. In Consideration to that, in accordance with the principles proclaimed in the Charter of the United Nations, recognition of the inherent dignity and of the equal and inalienable rights of all members of the human family is the foundation of freedom, justice and peace in the world, Bearing in mind that the peoples of the United Nations have, in the Charter, reaffirmed their faith in fundamental human rights and in the dignity and worth of the human person, and have determined to promote social progress and better standards of life in larger freedom.

Recognising that the United Nations has, in the Universal Declaration of Human Rights and in the International Covenants on Human Rights, proclaimed and agreed that everyone is entitled to all the rights and freedoms set forth therein, without distinction of any kind, such as race, colour, sex, language, religion, political or other opinion, national or social origin, property, birth or other status, to recall that, in the Universal Declaration of Human Rights, the United Nations has proclaimed that childhood is entitled to special care and assistance.

A galaxy of factors are cumulatively responsible for such catastrophe as such it convinced that the family plays a special and important role in a child's life, family as a system is embedded within system and not only is it a developing system but also the world in which it is embedded is ever changing. Each family member is a developing individual as the fundamental group of society and the natural environment for the growth and well-being of all its members and particularly children, should be afforded the necessary protection and assistance so that it can fully assume its responsibilities within the community, recognising that the child, for the full and harmonious development of his or her personality, should grow up in a family environment, in an atmosphere of happiness, love and understanding, considering that the child should be fully prepared to live an individual life in society, and brought up in the spirit of the ideals proclaimed in the Charter of the United Nations, and in particular in the spirit of peace, dignity, tolerance, freedom, equality and solidarity, with the development of self-esteem, self-confidence and sense of independence.

As to Keep in mind that the need to extend particular care to the child has been stated in the Geneva Declaration of the Rights of the Child of 1924 and in the *Declaration of the Rights of the Child* adopted by the General Assembly on 20 November 1959 and recognised in the *Universal Declaration of Human Rights*, in the *International Covenant on Civil and Political Rights* (in particular in articles 23 and 24), in the International Covenant on Economic, Social and Cultural Rights (in particular in article 10) and in the statutes and relevant instruments of specialized agencies and international organizations concerned with the welfare of children as indicated in the Declaration of the Rights of the Child, "the child, by reason of his physical and mental immaturity, needs special safeguards and care, including appropriate legal protection, before as well as after birth", the provisions of the Declaration on Social and Legal Principles relating to the Protection and Welfare of Children, with Special Reference to Foster Placement and Adoption Nationally and Internationally; the United Nations Standard Minimum Rules for the Administration of Juvenile justice (The Beijing Rules); and the Declaration on the Protection of Women and Children in Emergency and Armed Conflict. Recognising that, in all countries in the world, there are children living in exceptionally difficult conditions, and that such children need special consideration. Taking into due account of the importance of the traditions and cultural values of each people for the protection and harmonious development of the child, the importance of international co-operation for improving the living conditions of children in every country, in particular in the developing countries, as recognised in Convention on the Elimination of All Forms of Discrimination against Women (CEDAW) is also applicable to girls under 18 years of age. Article 16.2 of the Convention lays special emphasis on the prevention of child marriages and states that the betrothal and marriage of a child shall have no legal effect and that legislative action shall be taken by States to specify a minimum age for marriage.

The SAARC Convention on Prevention and Combating Trafficking in Women and Children for Prostitution emphasises that the evil of trafficking in women and children for the purpose of prostitution is incompatible with the dignity and honour of human beings and is a violation of basic human rights of women and children. The Government of India is addressing the protection of rights of children in India within the framework of the M.D.G.s, which India has committed to achieve by 2015. The Mid-Term appraisal report on the 10th Plan found that India is far from achieving the M.D.Gs as the outcomes on most of the goals were off-track in 2005. Child Rights and Millennium Development Goal summit International Society for Prevention of Child Abuse and Neglect.

The International Society for Prevention of Child Abuse and Neglect (ISPCAN), founded in 1977, is the only multidisciplinary international organization that brings together a worldwide cross-section of committed professionals to work towards the prevention and treatment of child abuse, neglect and exploitation globally. It could have spoken of the protection of human rights instead of their promotion. Today, Universal enjoyment of fundamental human rights is foremost among these conditions necessary for the realisation on international peace and understanding. The special feature of human rights struggle in the modern age is the universal respect for the first time in the International sphere.

- Whereas the United Nations has, in the Universal Declaration of Human Rights, proclaimed that everyone is entitled to all the rights and freedoms set forth therein, without distinction of any kind, such as race, colour, sex, language, religion, political or other opinion, national or social origin, property, birth or other status.
- Whereas the child, by reason of his physical and mental immaturity, needs special safeguards and care, including appropriate legal protection, before as well as after birth, whereas mankind owes to the child the best it has to give.

General Assembly

The Declaration as adopted by the General Assembly of the United Nations on 20th November 1959 reaffirmed faith on better standard of life in lesser freedom without any discrimination. The specialised agencies and international organizations concerned about the rights of the child, which establishes International standards for promotion and protection of the rights of the child, proclaims this *Declaration of the Rights of the Child* to the end that he may have a happy childhood and enjoy for his own good and for the good of society the rights and freedoms herein set forth, and calls upon parents, upon men and women as individuals, and upon voluntary organizations, local authorities and national Governments to recognise these rights and strive for their observance by legislative and other measures progressively taken in accordance with the following principles:

(a) *Principle 1:* The child shall enjoy all the rights set forth in this Declaration, Every child, without any exception whatsoever, shall be entitled to these rights, without distinction or discrimination on account of race, colour, sex, language, religion, political or other opinion, national or social origin, property, birth or other status, whether of himself or of his family.

(b) *Principle* 2: The child shall enjoy special protection, and shall be given opportunities and facilities, by law and by other means, to enable him to develop physically, mentally, morally, spiritually and socially in a healthy and normal manner and in conditions of freedom and dignity. In the enactment of laws for this purpose, the best interests of the child shall be the paramount consideration.

Affirming that mankind owes to the child the best it has to give and that the principle of 'the best interests of the child' should guide the actions of those responsible for them, the objectives offered a moral framework for Childs: these are enumerated below:

- To increase awareness of the extent, the causes and possible solutions for all forms of child abuse. To disseminate academic and clinical research to those in positions to enhance practice and improve policy.
- To support international efforts to promote and protect the Rights of the Child. To improve the quality of current efforts to detect, treat and prevent child abuse.
- To facilitate the exchange of best practice standards being developed by ISPCAN members throughout the world.
- To design and deliver comprehensive training programmes to professionals and concerned volunteers engaged in efforts to treat and prevent child abuse.

At this stage, special mention should be made of the extremely useful role played by UNICEF. Not only has this body worked actively for the universal ratification of the Convention, but it has also made a strong effort to promote its implementation. As UNICEF has begun to integrate the rights set forth in the Convention into its planning activities, its country offices are in turn incorporating the Committee's suggestions and recommendations in their programmes. UNICEF has also taken initiative to encourage and facilitate studies on subjects relating to the rights of the child, some of which have been carried out and complied by the UNICEF research institute in Florence, better known as Centre Innocents. This remains today the primary organization of the United Nations system responsible for International assistance to children. As remarked the International and National Framework against Child Abuse and/or Violence against Children is discussed below:

There are a large number of conventions and declarations related fully or partially to Child Protection from abuse and/ or violence. The most important are:

International-Framework over Child Protections

The UN Convention on the Rights of the Child and its Protocols

The UNCRC establishes numerous provisions for Child Protection from abuse and violence both in the public sphere and the private sphere.

Article19 States, that

(i) State parties shall take all appropriate legislative, administrative, social and educational measures to protect the child from all forms of physical or mental violence, injury or abuse, neglect or negligent treatment, maltreatment or exploitation, including sexual abuse, while in the care of parent(s), legal guardian(s) or any other person who has the care of the child.

(ii) Such protective measures should, as appropriate, include effective procedures for the establishment of social programmes to provide necessary support for the child and for those who have the care of the child, as well as for other forms of prevention and for identification, reporting, referral, investigation, treatment and follow-up of instances of child maltreatment described heretofore, and, as appropriate, for judicial involvement."– Article 28 (2) sets forth a child's right to be protected from corporal punishment in schools. Articles 32 through 36 articulate a child's right to protection from exploitation, whether economic or sexual. Other articles protect children from torture, capital punishment or life imprisonment, while still others promote the physical and psychological recovery of child victims of violence.

- Convention against Torture and other Cruel, Inhuman or Degrading Treatment or Punishment, 1984 and its Optional Protocol, 2002. International Convention for the Protection of All Persons from Enforced Disappearance, 2005 (opened for signature, December 2006).

- Protocol to Prevent, Suppress and Punish Trafficking in Persons, Especially Women and Children, supplementing the United Nations Convention against Transnational Organized Crime, 2000.

Legally non-binding resolutions and policies concerning violence against children have also been adopted by the specialised agencies and other entities of the UN system. These include resolutions adopted by the governing bodies of the *World Health Organization* and UNICEF. The executive committee of the Office of the United Nations High Commissioner for Refugees has also developed policies and guidelines related to the protection and care of refugee children.

The Convention on the Rights of Persons with Disabilities and its Optional Protocol was adopted on 13 December 2006 at the United Nations Headquarters in New York, and was opened for signature on 30 March 2007. There were 82 signatories to the Convention, 44 signatories to the Optional Protocol, and one-ratification of the Convention. This is the highest number of signatories in history to a UN Convention on its opening day. It is the first comprehensive human rights treaty of the 21st century and is the first human rights convention to be open for signature by regional integration organizations. It marks a paradigm shift in attitudes and approaches to persons with disabilities. With India signing the Convention and signalling that it will ratify it soon; laws in India will have to undergo a dramatic change. The convention describes discrimination on the basis of disability as any distinction, exclusion or restriction on the basis of disability which has the purpose or effect of impairing or nullifying the recognition, enjoyment or exercise, on an equal basis with others, of all human rights and fundamental freedoms in the political, economic, social, cultural, civil or any other field. It includes all forms of discrimination, including denial of reasonable accommodation.

The Convention is intended as a human rights instrument with an explicit, social development dimension. It adopts a broad categorisation of persons with disabilities and reaffirms that all persons with all types of disabilities must enjoy all human rights and fundamental freedoms. It clarifies and qualifies how all categories of rights apply to persons with disabilities and identifies areas where adaptations have to be made for persons with disabilities to effectively exercise their rights and areas where their rights have been violated, and where protection of rights must be reinforced. The convention is a blueprint to end discrimination and exclusion of the physically and mentally disabled in education, jobs and everyday life. No doubt some of the measures that India would have to take include anti-discrimination legislation, eliminating laws and practices that discriminate against persons with disabilities, and considering persons with disabilities when adopting new policies and programmes. Other measures include making services, goods and facilities accessible to persons with disabilities. The government would have to change its local by-laws and make it compulsory for buildings to be easily accessible to the disabled. Once the convention comes into force, a committee on the rights of persons with disabilities will monitor its implementation. Countries that ratify the convention will need to report regularly on their progress to the committee.

The Convention will benefit 650 million persons with disabilities around the world. It does not establish any new rights but rather emphasises and consolidates the existing rights and freedoms of persons with disabilities and the international commitments of States. The Convention defines disability as an element of human diversity and praises the contributions of persons with disabilities to society. It prohibits obstacles to the participation and promotes the active inclusion of persons with disabilities in society. The long-term goal of this Convention is to change the way the public perceives persons with disabilities, thus ultimately changing society as a whole.

For many years, disability related organizations and UN members have discussed and lobbied for the possibility of a convention specific to disabled people. Although existing human rights laws seem to provide equal rights for the disabled 10 per cent of the world population, the reality, in practice, is that these instruments have failed to protect the human rights and fundamental freedoms guaranteed to disabled people. Early initiatives did not receive too much attention, and it was not until April 2000 that the UN Commission on Human Rights invited the UN High Commissioner for Human Rights to examine measures to strengthen the protection and monitoring of the human rights of persons with disabilities in its resolution 2000/51. The General Assembly then established an Ad-hoc Committee (hereafter the Committee) in its resolution 56/168, in December 2001, on a Comprehensive and Integral International Convention on Protection and Promotion of the Rights of Dignity of Persons with Disabilities to consider proposals for a convention to protect and promote the rights of disabled people. Discussions at its first meeting included the underlying principles and a human rights based approach was preferred for this new convention.

Underlying Principles

A human rights perspective on disability means viewing people with disability as subjects and not as objects. It entails moving away from viewing people with disabilities as problems towards viewing them as holders of rights. Importantly, it means locating problems outside the disabled person and addressing the manner in which various economic and social processes accommodate the difference of disability and the disability rights is about ensuring the equal effective enjoyment of all human rights, without discrimination, it is inspired by the values that underpin human rights: the inestimable dignity of each and every human being, the concept of autonomy or self determination that demands that the person be placed at the centre of all decisions affecting him/her, the inherent equality of all regardless of difference, and the ethic of solidarity that requires society to sustain the freedom of the person with appropriate social supports. The article 3 of the Convention has stipulated the underlying principles of this convention as:

- Respect for inherent dignity, individual autonomy including the freedom to make one's own choices, and independence of persons.
- Non-discrimination.
- Full and effective participation and inclusion in society.
- Respect for difference and acceptance of persons with disabilities as part of human diversity and humanity.
- Equality of opportunity.
- Accessibility.
- Equality between men and women.
- Respect for the evolving capacities of children with disabilities, and respect for the right of children with disabilities to preserve their identities.

Key Provisions

The new Convention comprises fifty articles. Under Article 10, state parties are to guarantee that persons with disabilities enjoy their inherent right to life on an equal basis with others. They would ensure the equal rights and advancement of women and girls with disabilities (article 6), and also protect children with disabilities (article 7). They need to respect their homes and families. Children with disabilities would have equal rights, would not be separated from their parents against their will, except in their best interests, and would in no case be separated from their parents on the basis of a disability of either the child or the parents (article 23). The same article also talks about the elimination of discrimination relating to marriage, family and personal relations. Accordingly, persons with disabilities would have equal opportunities to experience parenthood, marry and establish a family, decide on the number and spacing of children, have access to reproductive and family planning education and means, and to enjoy equal rights and responsibilities regarding guardianship, wardship, trusteeship and adoption of children: all flowing from the equal protection and benefit of the legal principles.

The Convention also enjoins the State parties to prohibit all discrimination on the basis of disability, and take all appropriate steps to ensure that reasonable accommodation is provided (Article 5). In addition, they shall adopt appropriate measures to raise awareness throughout society, to foster respect for the rights and dignity of persons with disabilities and to combat stereotypes, prejudices and harmful practices relating to them (Article 8). Similarly, on the fundamental issue of accessibility (Article 9), the Convention requires State parties to identify and eliminate obstacles and barriers, and ensure that persons with disabilities can access their transportation, public facilities and services, information and communications. State parties are also obliged to ensure the equal rights of all persons with disabilities to live independently in the community, with choices equal to others, and shall take effective measures to facilitate full enjoyment by persons with disabilities of this right, and their full inclusion and participation in the community (Article 19). Persons with disabilities should be able to choose their own living arrangements, and have rights to protection against involuntary institutionalization.

According to the Convention, persons with disabilities have the rights to the highest attainable standard of health without discrimination on the basis of disability. They would receive the same range, quality and standard of free or affordable health services as provided to other persons and not be subjected to discrimination in the provision of health (Article 25). Countries must also guarantee freedom from torture, cruel, inhuman or degrading treatment or punishment, and prohibit medical or scientific experiments without the consent of the person concerned (Article 15) and protect the physical and mental integrity of persons with disabilities (Article 16).

Optional Protocol

India has not signed the optional protocol to the Convention and has even signalled its unwillingness to do so in the future. Signing the optional protocol would mean that the domestic situation of the disabled would become the responsibility of the international community. Accordingly, if all domestic avenues to enforce any of the convention rights have failed, an individual or an organization can approach the Ad-hoc Committee with an application. There is a mixed response to the decision of the Indian government, where some have expressed satisfaction with the confidence of the government of India to redress any grievances internally, others point out that such a procedure would have been useful in the case of non-implementation of the Convention.

National Policies and Legislations for Protection of Child Rights

Much legislation are made out to protect the interest of child and the State is required to ensure protection of children of tender age from abuse, and from entering vocations unsuited to their age and strength. The state is to further ensure that childhood and youth are protected against exploitation and abandonment and also to take measures to ensure free and compulsory education for all children till they attain fourteen years of age. The trafficking in human beings and forced labour, child labour is the root cause as a result of which children are deprived of their rights to free and happy home. So the rights of child can be protected with various measures which are discussed below:

Constitution of India

The Indian Constitution captures the essence of human spirit and celebrates the finest principles of equality, social justice and human dignity and guarantees rights to its citizens. All children in similar circumstances are required to be treated in a similar manner, and if not so treated, such treatment can be challenged on the ground of discrimination and arbitrariness. The attainment of social justice is one of the objectives of Constitution of India. Fundamental Rights and Directive principles of State Policy are intended to ensure socio-economic justice to all. The Constitution of India recognises the vulnerable position of children and their right to protection. Following the doctrine of protective discrimination, it guarantees in Article 15 special attention to children through necessary and special laws and policies that safeguard their rights. The right to equality, protection of life and personal liberty and the right against exploitation are enshrined in Articles 14, 15, 15(3), 19(1) (a), 21, 21(A), 23, 24, 39(e) 39(f) and reiterate India's commitment to the protection, safety, security and well-being of all its people.

The Constitution of India guarantees all children certain rights, which have been specially included for them .as such in articles 14 and 15. Article 14 provides that the State shall "not deny to any person equality before the law or the equal protection of the laws within the territory of India" but article 15(3) mentions that, *"Nothing in this article shall prevent the State for making any special provision for women and children"*. The State shall not deny to any person equality before the law or the equal protection of the laws within the territory of India; Article 15: The State shall not discriminate against any citizen on grounds only of religion, race, caste, sex, place of birth or any of them; Article 15 (3): Nothing in this article shall prevent the State from making any special provision for women and children.

(a) *Article 19(1) (a)*: All citizens shall have the right (a) to freedom of speech and expression.

(b) *Article 21*: Protection of life and personal liberty-No person shall be deprived of his life or personal liberty except according to procedure established by law.

(c) *Article 21A*: Free and compulsory education for all children of the age of 6 to 14 years.

(d) *Article 23*: Prohibition of traffic in human beings and forced labour Traffic in human beings and beggars and other similar forms of forced labour are prohibited and any contravention of this provision shall be an offence punishable in accordance with law.

(e) *Article 24*: Prohibition of employment of children in factories, etc. No child below the age of fourteen years shall be employed to work in any factory or mine or engaged in any other hazardous employment; Article 39: The state shall, in particular, direct its policy towards securing.

(*f*) That the health and strength of workers, men and women, and the tender age of children are not abused and that citizens are not forced by economic necessity to enter vocations unsuited to their age or strength.

(*g*) Those children are given opportunities and facilities to develop in a healthy manner and in conditions of freedom and dignity and that childhood and youth are protected against exploitation and against moral and material abandonment.

(*h*) The Indian Constitution provides in Article 39 that the State shall direct its policy towards securing: that the tender ages of children are not abused and that citizens are not forced by economic necessity to enter avocations unsuited to their age or strength.

(*i*) According to article 45, the state shall endeavour to provide within period of 10 years from the commencement of the Constitution, for free and compulsory education for all children below the age group of 14 years.

The Fundamental Rights embodies in Part-III and Directive Principles of state policy enshrined in the Indian Constitution provide the framework for child rights. The Constitution of India also provides for safeguards upon arrest, and states that a person should be produced before the nearest magistrate within twenty four hours of arrest. A juvenile in conflict with law or a child in need of care and protection should be produced before the competent Authority established under the Juvenile Justice Act, 2000 within 24 hours of having been picked up by the police and prohibits trafficking in human beings and forced labour. Several laws and national policies have been framed to implement the commitment to child rights. In order to achieve goals of social, economical and political justice, the Constitution of India guarantees special protection to the children against exploitation. Similarly, Part-IV of our national charter envisages many important provisions with regard to the welfare of the child workers. Article 47 also imposes a primary duty upon the state to raise the level of nutrition and the standard of living of its people and improvement of public health. The deep analysis of various provisions contained in our National charter makes it abundantly crystal clear that is the duty of the state to promote the welfare of the child workers and help them to grow into good citizens of the country. The state is required to ensure protection of children of tender age from abuse, and from entering vocations unsuited to their age and strength. The state is to further ensure that childhood and youth are protected against exploitation and abandonment and also to take measures to ensure free and compulsory education for all children till they attain fourteen years of age.

National Policies

The United Nations Convention on the Rights of the Child defines a child as "every human being below the age of 18 years unless under the law applicable to the child, majority is attained earlier". Biologically, a child is anyone in the development stage of childhood, between infancy and adulthood. The importance of the child lies in the fact that if there was no child, there was no humanity; moral sense of the society compels us to search for a solution to the problems of the children. In principle, every child has a right to love and beloved. Every society must, therefore, devote full attention to ensure that children are properly cared for and brought up in a proper atmosphere where they would receive adequate training, education and guidance in order that they may be able to have their rightful place in society when they grew up. Similarly Gabrial, Mistral of Chile, Nobel Prize winner poet, has rightly highlighted. "We are guilty of many errors and many faults, but our worst crime is abandoning the children, neglecting the fountain of life. Many of the things we need can wait. The child cannot. Right now is the time his bones are being formed, his blood is being made and his sense being developed. To him, we cannot answer, tomorrow.' His name is 'Today'. The peculiar position of the child arising from his physical and mental disability and position of dependence recognises the need for the special provisions in many matters and the law should take care of all this in the interest and general welfare of the child. The National Policy for Children Resolution, adopted in August, 1974, further developed the above ideas, and set out a policy framework and measures aimed at providing adequate services for children. These were to form a prominent part of the nation's plan for development of human resources free and compulsory education for all children up to the age of 14, provision of health and nutritional programmes and services, providing alternative forms of education for children unable to take full advantage of formal school education for whatever reasons – and measures for protecting children against neglect, cruelty and exploitation form part of the National policy for children.

The child has been subject of special laws and legal provisions. Because of its tender years, weak physique, and inadequately developed mind and understanding, it needs protection against moral and physical harm and exploitation by others, the child needs special care service to realise its full potential for growth and development. There are 300 central and state statutes concerning children. The major policies and legislations formulated in the country to ensure child rights and improvement in their status includes:

- National Policy for Children, 1974.
- National Policy on Education, 1986.
- National Policy on Child Labour, 1987.
- National Nutrition Policy, 1993.
- Child Prostitutes and Children of Prostitutes and Plan of Action to Combat Trafficking and Commercial Sexual Exploitation of Women and Children, 1998.
- National Health Policy, 2002.
- National Charter for Children, 2004.
- The Right of children to free and compulsory Education Act, 2009.

Underlying the National Charter for Children 2004, is the intent to secure for every child the right to a healthy and happy childhood, to address the root causes that negate the healthy growth and development of children, and to awaken the conscience of the community in the wider social context to protect children from all forms of abuse, while strengthening the family, society and the nation. These have been enacted with an intention to protect and help children and achieve the goal of child labour welfare enshrined in our National charter. This Charter has the following sections on child protection which lays special stress on the responsibility of the nation, for physical, mental, moral and special development of children. It is quite evident from the survey of various Articles of constitution, that our founding fathers had in their mind an intensive care to safeguard the workers from exploitation, improve their working conditions in various spheres. The subjects of child welfare, childcare and development have been enlisted in concurrent list of our Constitution.

- Survival, life and liberty.
- Protection from economic exploitation and all forms of abuse.
- Protection of the girl child.
- Care, protection, welfare of children of marginalized and disadvantaged communities.
- Ensuring child-friendly procedures.

(i) National Plan of Action for Children (NPAC), 2005

The National Plan of Action for Children was formed as a Department of Women and Child Development (now MWCD) in 2005. The Plan is being monitored by the Prime Minister's Office. The Action Plan aims at ensuring all rights to children up to the age of 18 years. It affirms the government's commitment towards ensuring all measures for the survival, growth, development and protection of all children. It also aims at creating an enabling environment to ensure protection of child rights. States are being encouraged to formulate State Plans of Action for Children in line with NPAC. The National Plan has identified several key priority areas that include children's right to survival, development, protection and participation besides monitoring and review of policies and programmes. The NPAC also stresses the need for budgetary allocations to achieve child protection goals.

- To regard the child as an asset and a person with human rights.
- To address issues of discrimination emanating from biases of gender, class, caste, race, religion and legal status in order to ensure equality.
- To accord utmost priority to the most disadvantaged, poorest of the poor and the least served child in all policy and programmed interventions.
- To recognise the diverse stages and settings of childhood, and address the needs of each, providing all children the entitlements that fulfil their rights and meet their needs in each situation the guiding principles of the NPAC 2005.

Enactment of Statute and Provisions of Law

So many laws were enacted by legislation for protection of child rights in India. National legislations for protection of child rights in the country are:

- Guardian and Wards Act, 1890.
- Factories Act, 1954.
- Hindu Adoption and Maintenance Act, 1956.
- Probation of Offenders Act, 1958.
- Bombay Prevention of Begging Act, 1959.
- Orphanages and Other Charitable Homes (Supervision and Control) Act, 1960.
- Bonded Labour System (Abolition) Act, 1976.
- Immoral Traffic Prevention Act, 1986.
- Child Labour (Prohibition and Regulation) Act, 1986.
- Prevention of Illicit Traffic in Narcotic Drugs and Psychotropic Substances Act, 1987.
- Pre-natal Diagnostic Techniques (Regulation and Prevention of Misuse) Act, 1994.
- Persons with Disabilities (Equal Protection of Rights and Full Participation) Act, 2000.
- Juvenile Justice (Care and Protection of Children) Act, 2000.

- Commission for Protection of the Rights of the Child Act, 2005.
- Prohibition of Child Marriage Act 2006.
- Domestic violence act 2005.
- Right to free and compulsory education Act, 2009.

Penal Provisions

The Indian Penal Code 1860 is a noble statute. So, some of the important penal laws are discussed below. Under this Act, some relevant sections have been discussed herewith:

(a) *Foeticide* (Sections 315 and 316).

(b) *Infanticide* (Section 315).

(c) *Abetment of Suicide*: Abetment to commit suicide of minor (Section 305).

(d) *Exposure and Abandonment*: Crime against children by parents or others to expose or to leave them with the intention of abandonment (Section 317).

(e) *Kidnapping and Abduction*:
  - Kidnapping for extortion (Section 360);
  - Kidnapping from lawful guardianship (Section 361);
  - Kidnapping for ransom (Section 363 read with Section 384);
  - Kidnapping for camel racing etc. (Section 363);
  - Kidnapping for begging (Section 363-A);
  - Kidnapping to compel for marriage (Section 366);
  - Kidnapping for slavery, etc. (Section 367);
  - Kidnapping for stealing from its person: under 10 years of age only (Section 369);

(f) Procurement of minor girls by inducement or by force to seduce or have illicit intercourse (Section 366-A).

(g) Selling of girls for prostitution (Section 372).

(h) Buying of girls for prostitution (Section 373).

(i) Rape (Section 376).

(j) Unnatural Sex (Section 377).

These aforesaid noble provisions are within the system, and despite these new legislations and conventions raise serious concerns for the safety of children and detrimental long-term effects. But it is quite unfortunate to describe here that the law dealing with sexual offences does not specifically address child sexual abuse. It is disconcerting but true, that Indian Penal Code 1860 does not recognise any kind of a child abuse. The law is silent on the rape of a male child. Only rape and sodomy can lead to criminal conviction. Any cause of action less than rape as defined under the law amount to outrage the modesty under Section 354 IPC. An offence under Section 354 IPC is a cognizable and bailable offence, which allows foreigners to simply leave the country before prosecutions begin. While Section 376 IPC seeks to provide women redress against rape, it is rarely interpreted to cover the broad range of sexual abuses, particularly of children that actually takes place, Section 377 has largely been used in prosecuting cases where anal and/or oral intercourse with children was involved. The punishment provided under sections 377 is imprisonment for life or imprisonment of either description for a term which may extend to 10 years and, shall also be liable to fine, Although it has been somewhat successful in penalizing child sexual abuse and complementing the lacunae of the rape law, but is woefully lacking in both scope of definition and category of sexual offence. There is a dire need to evolve more effective legal formulations as well as procedures to ensure that sexually abused children are offered the protection of the law and perpetrators are punished severely and unfailingly. The provisions relating to evidence and criminal procedure are not suited to deal with child sexual abuse. The adjudication of child sexual abuse cases has had a profound effect on law enforcement, prosecutors, and our nation's criminal courts, as the child abuse cases are problematic from several perspectives. In addition, these cases are often traumatic for the children involved and their families thereby representing considerable human suffering. In conclusion we can say that they are difficult to prosecute successfully and problematic for sentencing judges. Such cases also often require special attention. In responding these types of cases a considerable evolution has occurred in recent years. In the recent Supreme Court judgment in *Sakshi v. Union of India and others*, Hon'ble Mathur held as:

There is absolutely no doubt or confusion regarding the interpretation of provisions of section 375 IPC and the law is very well settled. Giving a wider meaning to section 375 IPC will lead to a serious confusion in the minds of prosecuting agency and the courts which instead of achieving the object of expeditiously bringing a criminal to book may unnecessarily prolong the legal proceedings and would have an adverse impact on the society as a whole. Therefore, it will not be in the larger interest of the state or the people to alter the definition of 'rape' as contained in section 375 IPC by a process of judicial interpretation as is sought to be done by means of the present writ petition. However, the judgment sought to reduce the trauma of the victim of child sex abuse or rape by laying some directions for the protection of the child victim of sex abuse or a witness to such an incident thereto. Female foeticide is primarily a legal issue referring to illegal killing of a foetus. In medical terminology, foeticide is termination of a foetus. It might occur during the initial stages of a legitimate induced abortion. However, the issue of foeticide normally assumes legal connotations in countries like India where female foeticide is on the rise alarmingly. In this context, cases of foetal homicide or foetal homicide are running rampant among the ignorant cross-section of people in India. Foetal homicide is as reprehensible a practice as other forms of violence against women, It is a shame for any progressive nation that a male child is given preference to a female child and consequently lives are literally nipped in the bud in front of the wide open eyes of an indifferent society.

The Pre-natal Diagnostic Techniques (Regulation and Prevention of Misuse) Act, 1994

This is an Act came into force on 1st January 1996 for the regulation of the use of pre-natal diagnostic techniques for the purpose of detecting genetic or metabolic disorders, chromosomal abnormalities or certain congenital malformations or sex-linked disorders, and for the prevention of misuse of such techniques for the purpose of prenatal sex determination leading to female foeticide and for matters connected therewith or incidental thereto.

The Juvenile Justice (Care and Protection of Children) Act, 2000

The Juvenile Justice (Care and Protection of Children) Act, 2000 is a comprehensive legislation that provides for proper care, protection and treatment of children in conflict with law and children in need of care and protection by catering to their development needs, and by adopting a child friendly approach in the adjudication and disposition of matters in the best interest of children and for their ultimate rehabilitation through various institutions established under the Act. It conforms to the UN Convention on the Rights of the Child, the UN Standard Minimum Rules for the Administration of Juvenile Justice (The Beijing Rules) 1985, the UN Rules for the Protection of Juveniles Deprived of their Liberty and all other relevant national and international instruments.

It prescribes a uniform age of 18 years, below which both boys and girls are to be treated as children. Clear distinction has been made in this Act between the juvenile offender and the neglected child. It also aims to offer a juvenile or a child increased access to justice by establishing Juvenile Justice Boards and Child Welfare Committees. The Act has laid special emphasis on rehabilitation and social integration of the children and has provided for institutional and non-institutional measures for care and protection of children. The non-institutional alternatives include adoption, foster care, sponsorship, and after care.

The following sections of the Act deal with child abuse:

- *Section 23:* Punishment for cruelty to juvenile or child: The Act provides for punishment (imprisonment up to six months) if a person having the actual charge of, or control over, a juvenile or the child, assaults, abandons, exposes or wilfully neglects him/her, causes or procures him/her to be assaulted, abandoned, exposed or neglected in any manner likely to cause such juvenile/child unnecessary mental or physical suffering.

- *Section 24:* Employment of Juvenile or Child for Begging: The Act provides for punishment (imprisonment for a term which may extend to 3 years and fine) if a person employs or uses any juvenile/child for the purpose or causes any juvenile to beg.
- *Section 26:* Exploitation of Juvenile or Child Employee: The Act provides for punishment (imprisonment for a term which may extend to 3 years and fine) if a person ostensibly procures a juvenile/child for the purpose of any hazardous employment, keeps him in bondage and withholds his earnings or uses such earning for his own purposes.
- *Criminal Procedure Code, 1973*: An alleged juvenile offender produced before Juvenile Justice Board is to be released on bail irrespective of whether the juvenile is accused of a bailable or non-bailable offence. A juvenile offender may not be released on bail if release will bring him into association with a known criminal or expose the juvenile to physical/psychological danger. The criminal procedure code, 1973 provides that a person under age has to be released on bail even in case of non-bailable offence, and at the time of investigation the police should not call him to police station for investigation to the station, but the child can give evidence as a witness before police as well as court. These remedial measures are available in India. Juvenile justice Act was amended in the year 2006 to protect the interest of the children/juvenile/delinquent abuses in adequate form for the welfare of the society.

Child Trafficking

Children are trafficked for several reasons including sexual exploitation; adoption; entertainment and sports (for example, acrobatics in circus, dance troupes, beer bars; as camel jockeys); marriage; labour; begging, organ trade, drug peddling and smuggling. Trafficking of children usually happens through well organized networks. Family, relatives, friends, community leaders, brokers, the pimps and owners of brothels, the police, political connections and the criminal nexus; all or any of these have been found to be involved in the process of child trafficking. Poverty, as a major reason responsible for trafficking in children, is not the only cause. Loss of traditional sources of livelihood, growing unemployment, forced migration, and growing consumerism resulting from globalisation have all contributed to the increase in child trafficking. The socio-economic situation and geographical location of the family add to the vulnerability. While both boys and girls are victims of trafficking, girls are more vulnerable, especially to trafficking for sexual purposes. This Act much more contributes about the trafficking.

The Immoral Traffic (Prevention) Act, 1956

In the year 1986, the Government of India amended the erstwhile Suppression of Immoral Traffic in Women and Girls Act 1956 (SITA), and renamed it as the Immoral Traffic (Prevention) Act (ITPA), 2000 to widen the scope of the law to cover both the sexes exploited sexually for commercial purposes.

In the Section 2(a)(a), Inclusion of Definition of Adoption, 'Adoption' means the process through which the adopted child is permanently separated from his biological parents and becomes the legitimate child of his adoptive parents with all the rights, privileges and responsibilities that are attached to the relationship.

Section 2(d)(i), Child beggars to be included in the definition of children in need of care and protection.

Section 10(1): In no case a juvenile in conflict with law shall be placed in a police lockup or lodged in jail.

Section 14(2): Since the provision for enquiry to be completed within four months lacks proper implementation, as inquiries are pending before the Boards for a long period of time, it is proposed that the Chief Judicial Magistrate/Chief Metropolitan Magistrate shall review the pending of cases of the Board every six months, and shall direct the Board to increase the frequency of its sittings or may cause constitution of additional Boards'.

Section 15(1) (g): The Juvenile Justice Board can make an order directing the juvenile to be sent to a special home for a maximum period of three years only.

Section 16(1): No Juvenile in conflict with law can be put under imprisonment for any term, which may extend to imprisonment for life Contravention of provisions dealing with prohibition of publication of name, etc., of child/juveniles shall be punishable with fine extending to twenty five thousand rupees as against existing 1000 rupees.

Section 4 and 29: The State Governments to constitute Juvenile Justice Board and Child Welfare Committee for each district within one year of the Amendment Act coming into force.

Section 33(3): The State Governments may review pending of cases before the Child Welfare Committee in order to ensure speedy completion of enquiry process.

Section 34(3): All State Government/voluntary organizations running institutions for a child/juvenile shall be registered under this Act within a period of six months from the date of commencement of the Amendment Act, 2006.

Section 41(4): State Government shall recognise one or more of its institutions or voluntary organizations in each district as specialised adoption agencies for the placement of orphans, abandoned or surrendered children for adoption. Children's homes and the institutions run by the State Government or voluntary organizations for children who are orphans, abandoned or surrendered shall ensure that these children are declared free for adoption by the Child Welfare Committee and all such cases shall be referred to the adoption agency in that district for placement of such children in adoption in accordance with guidelines.

Section 62(A): Every State Government shall constitute a Child Protection Unit for the State and, such units for every district, consisting of such officers and other employees as may be appointed by that Government to take up matters relating to children /juveniles with a view to ensure the implementation of this Act. The penalties for offences are involving children and minors. 'Child' under ITPA means a person who has not completed the age of sixteen years and 'prostitution' means the sexual exploitation or abuse of persons for commercial purposes. Section 3: Stringent action and punishment for keeping a brothel or allowing premises to be used as a brothel; Section 4: Living on the earnings of prostitution; Section 5: Procuring, inducing or taking a person for the sake of prostitution; Section 6: If any person is found with a child in a brothel it shall be presumed, unless the contrary is proved, that he has committed an offence of detaining a person in premises where prostitution is carried on, Section 6(1B): The punishment consists of imprisonment of either description for a term which shall not be less than 7 years, but which may be for life or for a term, which may extend to 10 years and shall also be liable to fine, with a provision for less than 7 years under special circumstances. In the Section 6(2A): A child or minor found in a brothel, on medical examination, detected to have been sexually abused, it shall be presumed, unless the contrary is proved, that the child or minor has been detained for purposes of prostitution or, as the case may be, has been sexually exploited for commercial purposes. Section 21: Establishment of Protective Homes by the State Government. Proposed amendments to the ITPA: under section 2(a) to raise the age of child from 16 to 18 years; Omission of the terms 'minor' and 'major' wherever they occur in the Act:

- *Section 3*: To enhance the punishment for a person who keeps or manages or acts or assists in keeping or management of a brothel.
- *New Section 5A:* To define the offence of "Trafficking in Persons" on the lines of International Protocol to Prevent, Suppress and Punish Trafficking in Persons.

- *New Section 5B*: To provide punishment for the said offence.
- *New Section 5C:* To provide punishment for a person who visits or is found in a brothel for the purpose of sexual exploitation.
- *Section 6*: To enhance the punishment provided for the offence of detaining a person in a premise where prostitution is carried on, section 10A to enhance the term of detention in a corrective institution from 5 to 7 years. In the section 13(2-5) confers the powers of Special Police Officer under this Act to the Sub-inspector in the place of Inspector of Police.
- *New Section 13A:* To constitute a Central Authority by the Central Government for the purpose of effectively preventing and combating the offence of trafficking in persons.
- *New Section 13B*: That empowers the State Government to constitute a State Authority for the purpose of effectively preventing and combating the offence of trafficking in persons; Omission of Section 20.
- *Section 22*: To make provision for in camera proceedings to protect the privacy and dignity of the victims.

Amendment of the Schedule to the Prevention of Money-Laundering Act, 2002 to make applicable the provisions of confiscation of the property of the persons involved in the offence of trafficking in persons. From the said Schedule, the entry relating to Section 8 of the ITPA is being omitted as a consequential nature. In concluding remarks it clearly justifies that Section 5 of ITPA1956 prescribes punishment for a term of not less than 7 years but may extend to life for inducing a child into prostitution, but does not directly address child abuse.

Child Labour (Prohibition and Regulation) Act, 1986

Every child is precious resource of the country. Children in India are less safe now, even if they are among their own. Violence against children has arisen in the country despite twenty-two laws and six national policies. According to a report the most important/Principal enactment/statute on the subject is "The Child Labour (Prohibition and Regulation) Act 1986. Acually the protection of child labour and his working condition began with the India Factories Act 1881, which restricts the working hours to 9 hours and minimum age of employment to seven years. In 1901, the mines Act prohibited the employment of children below 12 years in mines and other dangerous employment. In 1911 the Factories Act prohibited the employment of children during night. The factories Amendment Act of 1922 passed to implement the minimum age of employment to 15 years and maximum working hours to six. The comprehensive report of the Royal commission of Labour in, 1931 recommended extensive reforms like abolition of recruitment of child labour through monetary advance, minimum age to 12 yrs and 5 hours of work. The Employment of Children Act, 1938 prohibited the employment of children less than 15 years of age restricting the occupation in transport, railways, etc. In the International year of the child, the Ministry of Labour, Government of India, brought its resolutions for improvements. The Child Labour Regulation Act, 1986 came into existence on 23rd December 1986 with a purpose to eliminate child labour and provides for punishments and penalties for employing children below the age of 14 years in various hazardous occupations and processes. The Act provides power to State Governments to make Rules with reference to health and safety of children, wherever their employment is permitted. It provides for regulation of work conditions including fixing hours of work, weekly holidays and notice to inspectors, provisions for resolving disputes as to age, maintenance of registers, etc. Through a recent notification, child domestic workers up to 14 years of age working in restaurant, hotels and *dhabas* have been brought within the purview of the Act. It is one step towards the total elimination of child labour. In 1987 the Government of India adopted a new set of policies towards working by which Government would no longer ban child labour, but would instead seek to ameliorate the conditions of working children rather than to press for compulsory universal primary education. Poverty has a tremendous impact upon them; childhood is a period of life which should not be devoted to work but to education and development. According to the statistics provided by the Government of India, around 90 million out of 179 million children in the 6 to 14 age groups do not go to school and are engaged in some occupation or other. This means 50 per cent of children are derived from their free and happy livelihood. The highest numbers of children are found working in agricultural sector. The working conditions of children are inhuman and payment is too meagre. So it is the need of the hour take alarm about the situation and takes benevolent steps to do best for children.

Domestic Violence Act, 2005

Domestic Violence Act is such an Act which provide for more effective protection of the Rights of women and children guaranteed under the Constitution who are victims of violence of any kind occurring within the family and for matters connected therewith or incidental thereto. For the purpose of determining whether any act, omission, commission or conduct of the respondent constitutes 'Domestic Violence' under this section, the overall facts and circumstances of the case shall be taken into consideration. The noble Act specifically describes the child means any person below the age of 18 years and includes any adopted, step or foster child by virtue of domestic relationship including access to the shared household.

Nationwide studies reveal that as many as 3 million children witness parental domestic violence each year. Inter-family violence can cause serious, long lasting psychological harm to children, and, in many cases, it results in physical injury to the child as well. Parents who are abusive to one another sometimes intentionally injure their children in an effort to intimidate and control their adult partner. The assaults to the child can include physical, emotional and sexual abuse. Normalcy for a child growing up in violent home is distinctly different than what a child is nurtured in safe, loving and peaceful home although many parents believe they can hide domestic violence from their children. The children living in these homes report differently. Research suggests that between 80-90 – per cent of these children are aware of their parent's violence. Even if they don't see the actual fighting they hear the screams, see the bruises, broken bones, and abrasions and are directly affected by their parent's emotional pain and upset in the aftermath.

The Prohibition of Child Marriage Act, 2006

The Child Marriage Restraint Act, 1929 has been repealed and the major provisions of the new Act include, every child marriage shall be voidable at the option of the contracting party who was a child at the time of the marriage:

- The Court while granting a decree of nullity shall make an order directing the parties, parents and guardians to return the money, valuables, ornaments and other gifts received.
- The Court may also make an interim or final order directing the male contracting party to the child marriage or parents or guardian to pay maintenance to the female contracting party to the marriage and for her residence until her remarriage.
- The Court shall make an appropriate order for the custody and the maintenance of the children of child marriages.

Notwithstanding that a child marriage has been annulled, every child of such marriage shall be deemed to be a legitimate child for all purposes. Child marriages to be void in certain circumstances like minor being sold for the purpose of marriage, minor after being married is sold or trafficked or used for immoral purposes, etc. Enhancement in punishments for male adults marrying a child and persons performing, abetting, promoting, attending, etc., a child marriage is imprisonment up to two years and fine up to one lakh rupees. States appoint Child Marriage Prohibition Officers, whose duties include prevention of solemnization of child marriages, collection of evidence for effective prosecution, creating awareness and sensitization of the community, etc.

The Right to Education Act, 2009

The Right of Children to Free and Compulsory Education Act, 2009, popularly known as the Right to Education (RTE) Act, came into being in India from April 1, 2010. The act introduces a number of changes in education delivery through schools in India. Many of the changes are simply revolutionary, and if they are implemented properly well vastly improve the system of imparting education in the country. The Act is a landmark in the history of education related legislation in India. However, some of the provisions of the Act, although included with noble intentions, will have unintended consequences that might counter some of the advantages of the new system itself. The Right to Education Act mandates that unrecognised institutions which fail to meet the set criteria will have to close down after a period of about 3 years. However, it is mandatory that the students in these schools will have a right to seek transfer to other schools within the area. The act does not specify how and on what basis these students will be given admission in other schools. The Right to Education Act will be no simple matter either, the other shortfalls aside, the availability of funds and teachers remain significant roadblocks in the implementation of the Act. But the way the Act is currently structured, life in school after 14 will seem very difficult to a child. However, these following important points and sections contribute major changes to protect the educational welfare system.

- Decisions relating to screening and failing students (Section 16).
    1. Skill development.
    2. No feedback mechanism.
    3. Postponing development does not work.
    4. Inability to deal with failure.
- Prohibition on physical punishment and mental harassment (Section 17).
- No clear escalation mechanism. Only recognised schools allowed to function (Section 18).

- Unrecognised schools may be better than recognised ones. Unrecognised schools solve the problem of outreach. Prohibition of private tuition by teachers (Section 28).
- No Board examination in the period of elementary education (Section 30).

There are State Commissions for protection of Child Rights in every State and Union Territory. The functions and powers of the National and State Commissions will be to, examine and review the legal safeguards provided by or under any law for the protection of child rights and recommend measures for their effective implementation.

- Prepare and present annual and periodic reports upon the working of these safeguards.
- Inquire into violations of child rights and recommend initiation of proceedings where necessary.
- Undertake periodic review of policies, programmes and other activities related to child rights in reference to the treaties and other international instruments.
- Spread awareness about child rights among various sections of society.
- Children's Courts for speedy trial of offences against children or of violation of Child Rights.

As the State Governments, and Union Territories have provisions to appoint a Special Public Prosecutor for every Children's Court. Some states have, apart from these laws mainly concerning children; there are a host of related formulated state specific social legislations and criminal laws that have some beneficial provisions for legislation to deal with the care, protection and rehabilitation of children. Despite the above mentioned legislations, there are still major gaps in the legal provisions relating to child abuse in myriad situations, particularly in cases of trafficking, sexual and forced labour, child pornography, sex tourism and sexual assault on male children. The Ministry of Women and Child Development is therefore formulating a comprehensive legislation on Offences against Children.

In accomplishing the milestones, both at the national and international level, the non-governmental and civil society organizations have played an equally important role along with the Government in virtually every aspect concerning children. The media too has played a critical role in shaping public opinion and creating mass awareness. The Government of India and UNICEF collaborative initiatives over the years have focused on enhancing the capacities of the electronic and print media personnel in the Ministry of Information and Broadcasting so as to integrate and represent issues concerning children and their rights effectively. As a result, the media is gradually focusing on children's issues in a qualitative way. This is certainly a positive sign for the future and it is hoped that the media will increase its responsibility to include monitoring of child rights violations in a significant and persistent manner.

4 Socio-Legal Prospectus on Child Abuse

Child abuse is a phenomenon that has existed as long as families have existed. Every child is the precious resource of the country. The strength of a nation is reflected within all-round development of the children, who are destined to be successful citizens of tomorrow.[1] Childhood is a period of life that should not be devoted to work but to education and development. India is home to millions of indigent children. Many of them – all too often illiterate, sick, and malnourished – live in neglect with wretched families, who cannot take care of them. In a country like India with its multi-cultural, multi-ethnic and multi-religious population, the problems of socially marginalized and economically backward groups are immense. Within such groups the most vulnerable section is always the children.[2] Millions more are forced into the work force at the time; instead of that they should have to learn how to read and write. Millions still live in the streets as a result of the loss of their loved ones, the breakdown of their families, or simply because they no longer could endure the abuses inflicted upon them by parents, relatives, and employers. While this phenomenon is by no means new, globalisation and economic liberalization have in some instances aggravated the vulnerability of children. In India, where the staggering economic growth continues to produce scores of nouveau riches, the distribution of wealth has grown increasingly unequal. Such growth has certainly not reduced poverty, which continues to afflict hundreds of millions. Children are especially in difficult circumstances, unless tender plant is properly tended and nourished, it has little chance to growing into a strong and useful tree. The growth of the child into a mature and happy person with fully developed personality is largely dependent upon the support and attention as he receives from the society.

In our country today, there are a large number of children who are living in especially difficult circumstances and require attention of all stakeholders. Unfortunately not much is known to nature of the problems faced by these children or of the numbers involved, World Summit for Children and the World Declaration on the Survival, Protection and Development of Children to which India is a signatory, the Government of India through its National Plan of Action, for the first time, not only made a direct reference about this group of children but simultaneously devoted an exclusive section on them.[3] This apart, for the first time again, the section tried to spell out and bring together at one place all the different categories of children who were especially in difficult circumstances, such as the physically handicapped, mentally handicapped, those who are affected by drugs, victims of natural and manmade disasters are refugee children, street children, slum and migrant children, orphans, destitute and beggars, children suffering from HIV/AIDS, children of parents with HIV/AIDS and HIV/AIDS orphans, trafficked children, children of prostitutes and children forced into prostitution, children in conflict with law and children, whose labour is being exploited, many children live with disabilities.[4] An improved protection could be provided to them and the root cause which has led them to such situations could be deciphered too. There are other categories of vulnerable children too, like children affected by terrorism, insurgency and riots which could be added to this long list. Girl child, who have been victims of sexual abuse are another category that needs attention separately. The number of such categories of children is increasing day by day and because of their dispersed character, they have escaped the attention of policy-makers. Response to their needs has been ad-hoc and largely in the form of relief. It is important that such categories of children are identified, their problems studied and programmes developed whereby these children could be rescued and rehabilitated. There is a need to bring about improvement in the standards of service in most State run institutions and those run by voluntary organizations too. The best way to reach these children would be through non-institutional forms of care. Legal measures to protect these children are also necessitated. The problem of child neglect and exploitation in underdeveloped and developing countries is quite high and abnormal. Child abuse is shrouded in secrecy and there is a conspiracy of silence around the entire subject. In fact there is a well entrenched belief that there is no child abuse in India and certainly there is no sexual abuse or any abuse, which are meagre in records.[5]

In fact there are certain kinds of traditional practices which are accepted across the country either knowingly or un-knowingly, which amounts to child abuse. Existing socio-economic conditions also render some children vulnerable and more at risk to abuse, exploitation and neglect. As per the 'devadasi' custom, poor girl children from lower castes are dedicated by their parents to any deity or temple. In this case, they are sexually abused by those, who support this practice directly or indirectly. It is high time that we recognise this and take remedial measures. Lack of empirical evidence and qualitative information on the dimensions of child abuse and neglect makes it difficult to address the issue in a comprehensive manner.

The social aspects generally highlight the socio and economic conditions of the modern society which are responsible for the emerging of new crimes, which are called economic crimes. After Industrial revolution the economic crimes are increasing day by day. The other forms of child related crimes are in alarm at urban and rural bases in all corners of the society. Over Fifty per cent abusers were persons known to the child or in a position of trust and responsibility. Major findings of the study are: that, 53.22 per cent children reported having faced one or more forms of sexual abuse. Andhra Pradesh, Assam, Bihar and Delhi reported the highest percentage of sexual abuse among both boys and girls .21.90 per cent child respondents reported facing severe forms of sexual abuse and 50.76 per cent other forms of sexual abuse. Out of the child respondents, 5.69 per cent are reported to be sexually assaulted.[6]

Children on street, children at work and children in institutional care reported the highest incidence of sexual assault; more than 50 per cent abuses were by persons known to the child or in a position of trust and responsibility. Most children did not report the matter to anyone; as per the data outlined by The National Crime Records Bureau shows that cases of sexual offences against children have been on the rise from 2265 cases in 2001, the number has increased to 5749 in 2008, as conducted survey exposes that out of 12,447 children interviewed, more than fifty-three per cent reported having faced one or more forms of various forms of abuses.[7] The aim of the study was to develop a comprehensive understanding of the phenomenon of child abuse, with a view to facilitate the formulation of appropriate policies and programmes which are meant to effectively curb and control the problem of child abuse in India. The child abuse study is quite comprehensive, research oriented, educative and informative. The problem has been examined quite seriously and painstakingly right from ancient India to-date.

Historical Factors Influencing the Child Abuse

The major cause is man's materialistic attitude and the consequent erosion of values in our society. Man's cruelty to man has had no parallel. He has perhaps the dubious distinction of keeping members of his own species in perpetual bondage for his selfish and personal designs in a highly organized systematic manner. Human beings have exploited human beings for their purpose. Man has perpetuated this strategy for centuries and in the course of time elevated it to the status of trade, using his own kind as a commodity. This sort of treatment has not been confined to a particular land or territory. It remained a global concern for hundred and thousand years. The prevalence of child labour has been acute in periods of time, which varied in its nature and dimension, depending on the existing socio-economic structure of the society.[8]

In the past, child labour has been a part of the social organization in which all members pooled their labour to produce for the subsistence farming where the work of the child formed part of the labour necessary for the reproduction of the system and value of labour taken as a part of child's socialization for reproduction of the labour power. In this process children are subjugated and oppressed. Justice Bhagawati; poignantly describes that, they are non-beings exiles of civilization, living a life worst than that of animals, for the animals are at least free to roam about as they like and they can plunder or grab food whenever they are hungry but these outcastes of society are held in bondage, robbed of their freedom and they are consigned to an existence, where they have to live either in hovels or under the open sky and be satisfied with whatever little unwholesome food they can manage to get, inadequate though, it be to fill their hungry stomachs. Not having any choice, they are driven by poverty and hunger into a life of bondage, a dark bottomless pit from which, in a cruel exploitative society, they cannot hope to be rescued. Even today, human beings are ruthlessly shackled by their oppressors everywhere in the global scenario.

Violence and abuse is the behavioural tendency among the human race, our country is also not an exception to this habit of man. In our country too, this sort of exploitation exists in the name of 'beggar' it is known by different names in different regions. Names may be different but the ways of exploitation are by and large the same, the bonded labour system is a reflection of the economic and social deprivations that certain sections of our society have been suffering for generations.[9] The active become passive whether man wanted it or not, with slavery that reached its fullest development in civilization. It came as the first great split of society into an exploiting and an exploited class. This split has continued during the whole period. As regard child labour in ancient India, it can be said that it existed in the form of child slaves. Child slaves could be purchased or sold like commodities. To some extent, parent's obligations were very often involved in working for the landlord on such low wages that, it created conditions for the child to work on the farmer for wages and after remained as bonded labour in the landlord's house along with the parents to repay or to minimize the debt. In spite of that there was employment of children in agriculture and domestic service. The child labourers are not always entitled to a square meal and sometimes the diet actually varied according to their labour. The child labour is very common and could be witnessed in different occupations where they were engaged by the rich landlords to carry out activities directly or indirectly related to their agriculture sector.[10]

In the *Medieval Period,* a class of landless labourers came into existence, often bonded to the large landowners. These labourers used their children to help in their socio-economic activities. The rural artisan rarely worked alone. In fact, the entire family was a work unit with the 'Pater families' being the master craftsman. Occupations were determined largely on the basis of heredity, and children were introduced to their traditional craft at a young age. A workman's children can follow no occupation other than that of their father, nor can they inter-marry with any other caste. The persistence dominance of family-based work units indicates that, any disciplined organization of an industrial society was not in sight. Child labour in medieval India remained existence on a large scale and the rulers do not take any interest to weed out this practice and the result was that child was always exploited for this selfish ends.

In the *Modern Trend* the wake of unprecedented social change and development, the customary social values, family ties and community relationships seem to have got eroded, resulting in weakening of the traditional means of social control. While the economic growth has widened the opportunities for the satisfaction of our needs, it also opened up several illegitimate avenues in this respect. In modern age children have always been used in economic activities. Children had been employed in guild and in trade occupations, workplace was an extension of the home and work relationships are informal relationship. Work was a central aspect of their socialisation and training. This conception was changed with the advent of capitalism in the Industrialization during the modern period.[11] The new economy forces unleashed by capitalism destroyed the family based economy, a large number of labourers are displaced due to introduction of machines in agriculture sector. Many problems specifically concerning children assumed epidemic proportions. The desperate situation of the poor families forced children to live and work in the streets and supplement the family income in order to save themselves and their parents from starvation. Children those who are vulnerable to street life include those who have been abandoned by their families or sent into cities because of a family's intense poverty, often with hopes that a child will be able to earn money for the family and send it home. Children who run away from home or children's institutions frequently end up on the street since they rarely return home due to dysfunctional families, or physical, mental, and/or sexual abuse. In several areas of the country, disabled children are commonly abandoned, particularly in developing States. In addition, refugee children of armed conflict areas, children separated from their families for long periods of time, and AIDS orphans, repeatedly find nowhere to go but the street is the last resort.

The street children are under terrible stress and strain as for them it is a question of day-to-day survival. They are compelled to make adjustments to varied circumstances which might be changing almost every day. Hence adjustment to the social conditions becomes an important condition of survival in the streets. Homelessness and street life have extremely detrimental effects on children. Their unstable lifestyles, lack of medical care, and inadequate living conditions increase young people's susceptibility to chronic illnesses such as respiratory or ear infections, gastrointestinal disorders, and sexually-transmitted diseases, including HIV/AIDS.[12] Children fending for them must find ways to eat; some scavenge or find exploitative physical work. Many homeless children are enticed by adults and older youth into selling drugs, stealing, and prostitution.

Drug use by children on the streets is common as they look for means to numb the pain and deal with the hardships associated with street life. Studies have found that up to 90 per cent of street children use psychoactive substances, including medicines, alcohol, cigarettes, heroin, cannabis, and readily available industrial products such as shoe glue.

The mental, social and emotional growth of children are affected by their nomadic lifestyles and the way in which they are chastised by authorities who constantly expelled them from their temporary homes such as doorways, park benches, and railway platforms. The orthodox and notorious torture and violence inflicted on street children, many times escalating to murder – by police officers or death squads. Street children are in lack of security, protection and they struggle for survival. In the concluding observation for the present study that 30 per cent of the street children were subjected to child abuse. They were addicted to Gutakha (92%) and Tobacco (65.5%) they were working at a remote place from their house (48%) and were not getting adequate shelter (77%). History of previous schooling was obtained in minority (21%) and 6 per cent had step parents. Majority of them belonged to joint families (76%). They were not well entertained (80%), and were not satisfied with behaviour of their owner (77%). They were exposed to occupational hazards (40%) and majority of them (93.5%) had ambition to become good citizen in our country.

But, the extreme poverty made a possible situation in which the child had to be introduced in the labour market.[13]

Magnitude of the Problem

The parents of child labourers do not have positive attitude towards education of these teenagers, that is why diverting these working children towards education without consent and with consent of parent's is a challenging task. Due to poverty and illiteracy, these children are living in streets with poor environmental condition and are not health conscious. Family dispute and less love and affection by parents leads to hazardous habits of these children and most of them are exposed to occupational and health hazards. Most of the child does not get basic needs to fulfill their object; they work in hazardous place, lack of alternative employment, lack of education for children reinforcing this process. Besides, there was no compulsion on their part to get education up to a certain age limit and thus the children were left free to accept certain occupations even at a tender age. Therefore, the labour in this country was exploited by the employers for their benefits. Many children were employed in cotton and jute mills and coal mines. They were even employed for underground work. Children's position in mines was also not different. Their condition was very bad. It was dangerous to poverty exercises an adverse influence on the health and nutrition status of children. Inadequate and irregular earnings affect the quantity and quality of food that a family can consume throughout the year, its standard of living, and access and use of health care. The extent of poverty varies considerably between States, Orissa had the largest percentage of population below the poverty line and there is hardly any product in Orissa that has no child labour behind it. Moulding, Lock, Carpets, Bangles, Brick, Match box, Crackers, Wool and many other products have the invisible stamp of the toil put in by children caught in the web of poverty and exploitation in social system. Indeed, child labour in India comes cheap and easy.[14] Subject of child labour is often discussed in conferences, seminars and lectures and usually it is concluded that child and exploitation of child labour are deep rooted problems because of un-employment, poverty, over population, illiteracy and handling down of family trades. Hence the eradication of child labour is difficult rather impossible indeed. However, Law is a social engineering and it creates devices, machinery and means to reconcile the various conflicting interests in the society. The State has to implement the law according to the needs of the society. Society frequently faces pattern of changes. To meet up this situation, the new legislation(s) are being emerged and new dimension of laws are amended from time to time. The development in aid of technology, commerce vis-à-vis globalisation, liberalization, and industrialization, on increase with various fields like patent system, cyber space are certainly creating problems into the society. It is the duty and obligation of the State to find out the remedial measures in need to protect interest of the society. A State which is committed to such lofty ideals cannot favours the child labour which is psychologically disastrous, economically unsound and above all it is a social evil. It is the exploitation of childhood which constitutes, the most hideous and most unbearable to the human heart. Poverty is the root cause, which is fanning the flame of negligence to all types of children. To check this chronic ulcer, as such prudential legal measures are evolved too from time to time. Legislation(s) have come to the fore front to check the systems on the society. The rapid change in social life is the result of many factors. The fact lies with the subject that the modern society is not adjusted to the forces and motion of the present age. In other words the changes in law should be only in those directions and to that extent which is conducive for the society.

Social Legislation

Social change is primarily brought about by social legislation and it is necessary to devote some paragraphs about the nature and scope of social change. Whenever inequality exists in the society or social justice is denied to certain sections of the people, laws are enacted to bring about equilibrium, these laws may be designated as social legislation. Social legislation generally implicates public policy and it runs 'Like a red thread through the carpet of law'.[15]

Enactment laws and statutes various Acts, Rules and regulations have been aptly and dexterously taken into consideration for dealing as well as to control the social evils. It cannot tolerate that children are prevented from unfolding their potential by entering into employment at a tender age. It cannot bear that children are deprived of education, training and skill due to early participation of work force and thus emptied for future. It is important to note that however that changes in moral outlook and result that social action are condition precedent to effective social change it can therefore by no means denied that the theory and economic factors bring about a social change and other factor influence social conditions. There are some noble legislative enactment are able to check and balance the malice such as; The Mines Act, The Factories Act, Indian Mines Amendment Act, 1935 to regulate the working conditions and hours of work in mines. The factories Act was amended in 1935, and repealing and amending Act 1937. But do not alter any provisions for children, The Employment of Children Act, 1938 was enacted in order to prevent the evils of employment of children in workshops, which were not covered by Factories Act. The provision of this Act is continuing till now. This Act prohibits the employment of children under age group of 15 in Railway and Ports. By the amendment of 1939 the children with in age on 12 are prohibited to work in workshop connected with bidi-making, carpet-weaving, cement manufacturing, cloth printing, dying and weaving, manufacturing of matches, explosives and fireworks, mica cutting and splitting, shellac manufacture, soap manufacture, tanning and wool cleaning. It is fruitful to note that before independence the law relating to the employment of children in various sectors failed to achieve its goal to eliminate the social menace or to expose the evils of child labour.

The study discloses that first protective legislation for child labour was enacted in 1881. The Act prohibits the employment of children below the age of seven years; it limits their working hours to nine hours a day. The legislation aims at certain welfare measures for the welfare of child workers. In 1933, Children of pledging of labour Act 1933 was enacted with an objective to eliminate the evils arising from (pledging of labour) of young children by their parents for a loan taken in advance. Much legislation has been brought into existence in light of child labour welfare. Philosophy contained in our National Charter, the National policy for child labour, 1974 is a praiseworthy step initiated by the Government, which aims at the welfare of the child workers, so as to safeguard them against exploitation and enable them to grow into good citizens? The Shop and Establishment Act, are enacted in various States, the child labour (Prohibition and Regulation) Act, 1986 to prohibit the child in the work place is a dynamic enactment in this regard.[16]

The judiciary has almost brought a revolution in the life of child workers in India. The judiciary has always given a lead to save the child workers from exploitation and improve their working conditions. Besides Constitutional provisions, there are at present various legislative enactments and amendments for protection of the child, which provides legal protection to children in many more occupations. This above subject clearly highlights the socio-legal aspects of child maltreatment, exploitation, abuse and neglect on children in various sector of India. State governments are also equally responsible with the cause of the poor child workers and are busy to curb the arbitrary powers of the employers of the children in their establishment; moreover the policies are in force to check the abuse practice of child employment in various regimes. Economic reasons are the impelling forces that drive childhood for employment. As long as poverty is allowed to grow unchecked child labour will continue to expand. Without articulation on the social and economic dimensions on poverty, it is an impossible task to check child labour. The economic compulsions were arising out of unemployment. The rural poverty, landlessness, indebtedness, caste system and social customs, social practices like caste hierarchy, slavery bonded labour, sati, deva-dasi, un-touch ability, dowry system and other forms of abuse and exploitation, child neglect, on children were once accepted and fully practised by the society.[17] They have now been questioned and challenged by the present day society in the changing context of social order in the welfare of society. Child labour cannot be eliminated. The labour problem is a part of the general problem of human welfare. In many part of the state Orissa, as working categories of children particularly in domestic services, traditional, agricultural and also informal sectors. It is the primary object of the study is to highlight the research aspects *i.e.,* child abuse in the State of Orissa, therefore, without touching the Nature, establishment, areas of the geographical location, the socio-economic, cultural conditions and environmental aspect, it is impossible to highlight the vital factors and sources responsible for assessment about the survey on child abuse. There is a rationale thought for dignity of child liberty and equality which are considered a more important than before. The system and process itself. It is a stigma over the human society. Most of the studies in legal aspect, hitherto conducted were confined only to text-books and law reports in the library. This in house traditional and manual legal research cannot meet the complex, socio-economic problems at the society. The social and economic contexts of the law were not utilised but articulated on the basis of criticism. The socio-economic conditions of the modern society are responsible for the development of new incidents and legal wrongs, which are generally viewed as crime. The crime and economic crimes were increasing day by day to obtain and access easy money. On an average, family size ranges between 7 and 9 members. Poor housing with lack of basic amenities creates a physical environment that results in downtrodden amenities. Poverty is that condition in which a person, either because of inadequate income or unwise expenditure, does not maintain a scale of living to provide for his physical and mental efficiency and to function usually according to the standard of the society on which he is a member. The intensity and severity of poverty are also high in this region of the state. Apart from this, in the coastal province fishery is another important economic activity and a means to livelihood.

In India among other backward states has 80 per cent of its population are dependent on agriculture, the only livelihood and the alternative is mass migration to neighbouring States as Andhra Pradesh, Chhattisgarh, Gujarat, Madhya Pradesh and Maharashtra. Migration of impoverished families from rural areas to the cities is often the first step in those processes. A contributing factor is the disintegration of the family and its abandonment by the father that may be followed with frustration of unfulfilled expectations. In this critical juncture, such children's have been directly targeted in conflict situations. The lives of migrant children continue to be hampered by language and cultural differences, legal and social prejudice and marginalization by both teachers and other students. The migratory cultures and remote locations make it difficult for the existence. The general conditions of children are badly affected and encompass many types of disadvantages.[18]

It is true that, poverty is concentrated in rural areas and with in agriculture Poverty is also found to be higher and more widespread in those areas, where the local resource base particularly land, water and forest has been degraded, neglected or subject to over exploitation and subject to natural disaster. The landless person is a non-person. He is a faceless biped animal having no social significance in the society. To investigate the reasons as to how some of the land less house hold, many have lost their land due to indebtedness, manipulation by land lords and eviction. The dalita families, do not have own land or other means of livelihood despite their predominance as agricultural labourers, which pushes them to migrate to the cities in search of work. Once here, they have no access to the provisions of citizenship – most often they do not get registered under the BPL provisions; housing in secure and protected areas is not possible; basic amenities of water, electricity and sanitation are often not accessible; there is no ICDS centre where children can be sent to for pre-school education,[19] there are limited educational opportunities and poor access to basic nutrition or health care; and they have no access to the protection of the local *thana* or panchayats. In short, they become internal refugees, devoid of citizenship rights in the slums and urban poor areas, a doubly excluded status. Children from disadvantaged groups often endure poor living conditions; still they work to obtain basic needs and struggle for existence.

Domestic Worker

It is quite unfortunate that their need and willingness to work at low rates, without proper recorded status in private homes and public places, renders them vulnerable. The women are lured with promises of work and their vulnerable situation forces them to agree without any assurance of security and without the possibility of any bargaining for better provisions. The institutional mechanisms meant to set standards for work, labour, basic amenities, or protection fail to do so because they are not designed for a population that is outside the purview of society, especially for the excluded sections. Neither official estimates nor policies related to child labour take cognizance of the domestic worker. A large proportion of girl child labourers enter into unorganized sector of domestic work. Girls are seen as natural domestic workers, seemingly trained at home in doing housework. In the absence of official sources of data, rough estimates available from sporadic studies (again, data is difficult to procure from employers of Child Domestic Workers who often hide the facts) actually limit a realistic assessment of the magnitude and nature of the problem. However, that there is an overwhelming 'feminization' of domestic work is well established and visible. In Orissa, a study by the Department of Applied Economics of Vani-Vihar, Utkal University, reveals a strong preference among employers for girl-children, particularly part-time Domestic Workers.[20] Invariably, all research points to the fact that Child Domestic Workers are preferred, not only because they cost less but are more pliable.

The Utkal University study found that nearly 90 per cent of Girl Domestic Workers started work before they completed 12 years of age. More than 75 per cent belonged to the age-group 12-14 years. Pre-puberty girls are becoming targets of sexual abuse because due to unawareness of their sexuality. Sexual abuse among the domestic workers are increasingly; 70 per cent stepped out to work to supplement the family income, the remaining 30 per cent did so owing to family breakdowns – either the father had deserted the family, or he was an alcoholic or a drug addicted Or, the mother was living with another man. The Orissa study found that the absence of a supportive family structure made girl Domestic Workers more vulnerable. The study also found instances where mothers had accepted 'silence money', following the abuse of their daughters. This is often prompted by a sense of helplessness and ignorance with regard to registering official protests at the sometime fear of stigma arising out of social protest.

One common aspect is the mindset on Child Domestic Worker's that, their work hours extend to all hours; that they have no legitimate rights. Abuse, even sexual abuse, is accepted as a professional hazard to be endured. The only alternative is to leave the job. To the last one, all Child Domestic Workers are hesitant to talk about their jobs even after they have left them. They fear they will not only lose their present jobs but will be 'branded' by the local employer community.[21]

A study by 'Campaign Against Child Labour (CACL) in 2001' on child Domestic Workers in Orissa found that lack of regular income by the head of the family – mostly daily-wage earners or small cultivators, and fathers addicted to liquor – was a major reason for the incidence of child domestic labour. Intense poverty in backward areas where alternative avenues for earning are non-existent is widely acknowledged as being responsible for the practice of Child Domestic Workers.[22]

The National Convener of C.A.C.L., at Orissa, Mr. Ranjan Mohanty stated that, it is very difficult to get authentic data on sexual abuse of Domestic Workers. He says: "More than 90 per cent of girl-children engaged in domestic worker were exploited through different forms of sexual harassment by their employers, or by their cousins or relatives "Often, man (malika) 'Owner' will ask domestic workers to massage their bodies and nobody thinks anything about it. Even male domestic workers are sexually abused," it is found that out of 70,000 sex workers, 15 per cent had begun working as Domestic Workers between the ages of 15 and 18. All such cases of Child Domestic Worker exploitation and abuse that come to light are seen against the backdrop of 'backward' villages or small towns. But this does not mean that abuse on sexual or otherwise to Child Domestic Workers is common within the households of those holding power and office. Poverty may be these children's overt enemy, but the covert perpetrators of these crimes are people with moral indifference.[23]

There is no precise statistics available on the number of sexually abused and exploited children-inevitably so, given the sensitivity of the issue, the criminal and covert nature of these violations and limited research that has been conducted. Judicial verdict about protection of child *i.e.*, Honourable Supreme Court passed an order, the central government 'Amended' the All India Service (Conduct) Rules 1968, in February 2000. This prohibits the employment of children below the age of 14 as domestic servants by government employment. In Orissa, it is promptly implemented from 10th October, 2006.[24] But the practice is rampant and working in homes are common, in every days news in print media and electronic media, there must be a report about child abuse and exploitation, the Government is escaped to say that various social organization or NGOs do their best to find out the child labours, who is abandoned. But it is quite difficult in the state of Orissa from district to district and location to destination to collect data for this project. So researcher find some observations as such that, in the State of Orissa there are various reasons are come to forefront that the children's are deprived from their basic need and object. There are various categories of children face many problems when they are out of home in search of a work. These are street children, working children, deprived children, juvenile in conflict with law, and the slum children are those who live in the most overcrowded and unhygienic place of environment. It is a curse to their livelihood. Let's begin with few observations on the distinctive status of children in society and its responsibility towards child survival, protection and development. It is the bounden duty of a State to ensure that every child is adequately housed, clothed, fed and trained, so that they may able to enjoy the pleasures of childhood. It is incumbent upon a nation to make sure that each and every child gets the optimum conditions for its growth enabling thereby its survival, protection and development. The social reality, however, is a different tale to tell. What happens always in human society in our relationship towards the society around us, which may be called as a double reality; the normative system embodying what ought to be differs much from the factual order embodying what is. Though these two orders cannot be completely identical, perhaps they are not as much strikingly desperate in any other case as in the case of the treatment meted to the child. Due to developments such as these, the standard and treatment of children has reached a point where child maltreatment as a discrete 'problem' came to be identified.

Socio-economic Strata

Today, there can be little doubt that the abuse and neglect of children are significant issues for both policy and science. Child maltreatment and neglect pave the way for significant issues for current policy and research. Most of the families who live in slums belong to lower socio-economic strata. More (most studies put the figure at 60%)[25] girls than boys living below the poverty line are deprived of an education and are sent out to work to supplement the family income. In the growth of the cities in the State of Orissa without proper planning, care and caution for urban slum's peoples for their health and prosperity. Street children are by-product of urban slum, so their health condition is generally poor.

Hygienic Conditions

People's health condition are very much deplorable generally they suffer with malnutrition as well as transmittable diseases like scabies and tuberculosis because of despicable living conditions that are unsanitary and very cramped (hence close proximity to their peers). A large number of these children are mentally, physically and sexually abused. Many may suffer from chronic diseases like TB, leprosy, typhoid, malaria, jaundice and liver/kidney disorders, Scabies, gangrene, broken limbs and epilepsy are common, Venereal disease is rampant among older ones (14 yrs+).[26] HIV and AIDS cases are now widely seen. Most street children are exposed to dirt, smoke and other environmental hazards. They are constantly exposed to intense sun, rain and cold. Though there are supposed to be 'free' Government/Municipal Hospitals in all cities, street children do not have easy access to them due to the need to pay bribes to enter, or the indifferent or hostile treatment meted out to them by the staff. Bhubaneswar, Berhampur, Cuttack report extreme conditions in this regard. There are thousands of Street children (male and Female, the males being more visible) who spend a major portion of their time living and/or working on the street, disconcertingly visible, yet uncared for, unprotected, often ignored, even shunned. For many such children the street has become their home. In our State Orissa, these children are seen for rag picking, selling lottery tickets at day lights polishing shoes, hawking newspapers, peddling various items on the pavements or guarding parked cars. Other street children make their living through pretty theft, prostitution, begging, selling sundry items of spurious origins on the pavements, peddling drugs, or just hanging around. No matter what the correct number the fact remains that in the State of Orissa there are countless street children is still remain. Ganjam district is also a district in the State of Orissa has no exceptions to it, the city Berhampur is a city which is the heart city located in southern Orissa, have also countless street children, male and female, growing in number from year to year. Therefore million children are living in the streets struggle hard for their survival:

Children living on the streets are especially vulnerable to victimization, exploitation, and the abuse of their civil and economic rights. Territorial indifference and geographical problem have led to continual neglect and abuse of these children. These are out lined below as follows:[27]

1. The increasing population of street children.
2. The perception of street children as criminals, and the lawlessness of police.
3. The lawlessness of police:
   (a) There has been a marked acceleration in urbanization over the past two decades. If the present trends continue, urban population may account for about one-third of the total population by the turn of the century.
   (b) Street children learn to cope with life on the streets very quickly. They learn to live off the street.

The following is a list of activities and occupations undertaken by street children for their sustainability; as like collecting and selling waste paper, plastic, scrap metal, cleaning cars and two-wheelers, selling water, sweets, biscuits, clothes, selling newspapers and flowers on streets, making and selling flower garlands, begging, pimping, pick pocketing, stealing etc. Working in roadside stalls or repair shops, coolie work or working in small hotels (kitchens etc.). The most common and pervasive form of abuse over street children is experience by the police 'State agency'. They force them to clean the stations, deploys them for their miscellaneous work, they beat them, they take money from them, and they torture them into confessing to crimes or to name who committed them. The average age of street children is: 33 per cent among 6-10 yrs, 40 per cent 11-15 yrs, and 27 per cent 16 yrs + are common age groups in various cities of Orissa. 80 per cent of the working children in urban cities are migrants, living without their families. Out of that 36 per cent of children are in the Zari, glass industry, and rest of children working in the Kaju, Kewada, Maham, Brick industries and other small scale projects and local manufacture companies in Berhampur city. These Street children can be found easily in work condition at Berhampur in cottage industries, carpet factories, hotels and restaurants, *dhabas, halwai* shops, automobile and engineering workshops, building and construction, brick making, garbage collection, forestation, Cattle grazing, agriculture, mining operations, weaving, book binding etc. Many of the children are engaged as domestic servant too. Most street children find themselves some work, even though they may not be steady and lose jobs regularly. Many think of rag picking as a 'job'. A study shows that 39.3 per cent working children are paid inadequately, and 34 per cent complain of being forced to overwork.[28] Many children are lured into bonded work or 'work-camps' that they are unable to escape from, due to unscrupulous and cruel proprietors or middlemen. Corporal punishment ranges from hand beatings to hitting with metal rods every time they make a single mistake. Similarly a number of children are also engaged in a number of other livelihood activities in subsistence sector. A large number of these children are not paid any wages on a regular basis on the plea that they are being trained, which increases their dependency on their employer. The following problems are embodied to an observation by the researcher in the various parts of benevolent work. Numerous reality and face of the problem glamour with reasons thereon.

Stark Reality's of Street Children

The reality of the street child is the naked and vicious face of poverty, sickness and exploitation. The tragedy is, that those who bear it are themselves innocent, lonely and frightened young children. Street Children are those unfortunate children who basically: Have only intermittent contact with parents or family (usually mother or sisters) but live most of the time with other street children in the city streets, or are on the move. There are numerous reasons for a child to leave home. They have been literally abandoned by their parents/relatives, found themselves on the street from the beginning because of family problems, or have chosen to leave home due to some kind of constant abuse. Those who have run away from home can further be separated into two categories:[29]

(i) Those who have an unpleasant or traumatic home environment.

(ii) Other community base problem. 'Religion' plays a vital role in the communal sphere.

Religion of street children in India varies greatly according to area or location but, in general, approximately 70 per cent are Hindu, 18 per cent are Muslim, Christian and others. Percentage of Hindu children is as high as 82 per cent in City Berhampur, Aska, Bhanjnagar (almost 50 per cent of Hindu children belong to scheduled caste or tribes and other *dalit* class peoples of our state.) Maximum street children are boys. Girls are more difficult to trace but they are, 'by far' the most vulnerable. Street children learn to cope with life on the streets very quickly. They learnt to live off the street. These are the worst form of practices carried by the children as a regular profession to win the bread and butter for them and their family. They have not seen the reality of their perspective and gloriousness of human life. They haven't any knowledge of their mankind right, which is an inalienable right and sacrosanct right of a human being.[30]

In the State of Orissa tribal problems are innumerable in every sphere as to complete the various aspects of the children, it is necessary on the part of the project to highlight the events of tribal community and district profile to find out the reality. In this tribal district with a low literacy rate, the parents of the street those children are illiterate and even up to the extent of complete illiteracy in almost all or 95 per cent in ratio, They are neglected by and isolated from society, excluded from government policy, deprived of services, exposed to the elements, subject to physical danger and exploited by unscrupulous adults on the street, in many cases even by the police.

Street children, still remain an unsolved problem in the developing States. This phenomena lag behind in their socio-cultural, psychological, physical and mental development in comparison to normal children. Hence, this study has been under-taken to find out the socio-cultural background, socio-legal analysis, ecological factors and various problems faced by these children. This cross sectional study conducted in and around Berhampur city included some of street children chosen randomly to find out the pure theory of the subject. After obtaining a detailed history regarding their caste, profession of their parents' family and environmental history, a detailed assessment of child labour was done. Special emphasis was laid upon child abuse, factors responsible for compelling them to adopt child labour and life style of these children. All of them were subjected to physical examination and signs of occupational hazards. Data analysis was done. In the collection from various studies, it purports that the street children were subjected more frequently to child abuse, were addicted to Gutakha and tobacco and were working at a remote place from their house and not getting adequate shelter. They experience family problems which they are unable to solve: *i.e.*, alcoholism, child abuse, ill treatment by stepparents, unemployment and poverty.[31]

Their tolerance level has been far exceeded, leading to the drastic decision to leave their family. Those who have run away from home, who wanted to study work but were not allowed and came to experience the exciting experiences of city life, glamorized by magazines and movies. They were not well entertained and were not satisfied with their owner's attitude. They were exposed to occupational hazards, deficiency diseases. Working children are common problems of developing cities like ours, it's eventually impairs the personality and creativity of Children. They always desired to be secured in every respect. In literature most of the workers have reported physical abuse as a very important finding in child mal treatment. They have reported that even this maltreatment is so aggressive that at times children run away from homes. These findings are also supported by NCRB report 2009.[32] Regarding sexual abuse most of the workers have a common opinion that, it is under reported. As such to gain confidence over the child labour it needs a complete visualization on the spectrum of the iceberg about all abuses which is the need of hour.

Tourism and Growing Phenomena

Children's were being an indispensable bit of every civilized society, as tourism brings wealth, promotes universal kindliness and also maintains good friendly relations between host and tourist countries. There are enough instances in ancient Hindu literatures where guest were honoured and respected by the host. In those days in the name of the development much priority has been given to the tourism sector Government thought that promotion of tourism is the prosperity of the Nation that's why tourism is gaining high priority in the development policy of various developed countries but the Government turns blind eye towards the incidents activities which are illegal in nature are offence in the eyes of law.

Over the years, in India, pilgrim tourism forms an important sector of development; it is a serious concern about the menace in our society. No doubt trafficking of children for sex tourism has now become a global phenomenon but third world countries are the prime destinations of child sex tourism. India has no exception to it. In the place of Tourism, sex is one of the most vicious flash trade to that, millions of children from all over the world are dragged into the site to fulfil their hidden goals. Research in pilgrim sites finds concrete facts for lust. Unconditional tourism promotion is that in indeed promotes exploitation in various forms. Trafficking in women and children is a complex and multifaceted phenomenon blended with sex tourism. Tourist destinations are yet other sites where sexual exploitation of children has been observed.

Pilgrim Tourist Sites

The sites which are most conducive environment for child exploitation are as follows:

- Coastal sites.
- Heritage sites.
- Various forms of accommodations.
- House boats.
- Home stays.
- Hotels, lodges, Dhabas, Areas on street corners, beach, deserted.
- Construction sites, playgrounds, parks, cinema theatres, local.
- Prostitution houses, railway station, stadiums cemetery.

This study depicts that even Indian tourist exploit children. Whatever may be the reasons for the growth of child sex tourism but it is a fact that children are coerced, forced and tricked into the sex-trade which is rampant and common in every time on the place of destination.[33]

All forms of commercial sexual exploitation are exclusively summarized by the author to distinguish it from one another in its form these are categorically outlined the stark reality. It is reflected that all items of the supermarket purchased by the customers as an article or treated as marketable commodity. Child prostitution, Child Trafficking, Child sex tourism, child pornography and abuse of boy Childs, Non-commercial forms of exploitations, etc., are rampant in our society. In fact certain cases are unreported and hidden shrouded behind a veil of silence due to exposure of social portfolio. The factors responsible for making children vulnerable to exploitation of children are in the forms of:

- Child abuse.
- Child trafficking.
- Child prostitution.
- Child pornography.
- Child sex tourism.
- Child labour.
- Child marriage.

All these in turn increase vulnerability of children to drugs, crimes, HIV/AIDS,[34] and alienation from communities and families. It is also a belief in the mind of tourists that sex with children is safe and having sex with virgin children will cure HIV/AIDS land other sexually diseases, it is believed by foreigners that the traditional healing mechanism. As a result of that they are eager to practice the same to achieve the object in this manner. The Foreign tourist who comes with the intention of exploiting children mostly stay in the hotels which are near slums or poor areas and claim that sex between a young girl and an adult male will improve his business prospects or bring good luck to the adult males. Sex with a young virgin is claimed to be a cure of HIV and other transmitted diseases. This type of traditional healer practice is also responsible for the abuses of children and to have sex with a minor as a form or treatment. Those types of abuse are remarked as non- commercial forms of child exploitation. One thing is fact that the children have been abused in various forms which is a complete curse for the child community.[35]

A field study conducted in tourist destinations of the east coast sites which depicts that majority of these children came from families affected by poverty, unemployment, and increasing crimes against children in developing countries leave an impression in the mind of for feigners that child in particularly at India and inside the country most of the children are vulnerable and any one can be exploited very easily for commercial sex but within the State of Orissa having sex with wide range of tourists those who mat pay just Rs. 50/ up to tourists who pay Rs. 200/ per day primarily in demand as less risk with male children selling sex than girls due to social stigma and fear of Pregnancy. In case of Child sex tourism, it is boys who are mostly exploited in Puri and surrounding areas. Most of the foreign tourists use hotels while domestic tourists use small lodges and rooms in the bars for this purpose, newly set up massage units and parlours also cater solely to tourist demand. Foreign tourists also come into contact with children in the guise of 'English teacher' or

'Social worker'. Few hotels are provided with accommodation only to foreigners to practice their business prospects in smoothly manner to fulfil the greed. The discrimination prevails in every sphere in the society in need of competition.[36]

Tourists have to give an option about the male and female children which has assumed a serious dimension and this critical juncture. No doubt so many coastal areas faced difficulties due to reduction of the fishing industry. Boys were employed in restaurants, hotels and tourist shops near the beach and conducted prostitution as an adjunct. Few acted and deployed as tourist guides. Majority of the study samples were outlined in the findings as under on 12 years of age. Exploiters included foreign tourists, long-term foreign residents, local men, migrant workers and seamen, these peoples involvement of the community in exposing and ostracizing persons indulging in or aiding and abetting child sex is very important as it will lead to the shifting of the stigma from the accuser to the accused. It is difficult to know the magnitude of the problem because of their secret nature of trafficking. It is not an easy to find the location, where the activities are purposefully used as service centre to fulfil the aspirant's goal. No doubt the child sex tourism is very sensitive issue in this juncture but the relevant issues are conceptualising the theme for better finding. These are enumerated below:

(a) The issue is complex, sensitive and invisible.

(b) Not much research to prove the vulnerability of male children in sexual exploitation and abuse but the boys are abused in the pilgrim site is also high. Under pressure of commercialism children have changed from being subjects and are being made into objects.[37]

This clearly shows that the rights of children are neglected in various aspects which is sad to point out that only sex tourism is not the stigma but also other forms including various risks that, minors face those are online include sexual solicitation, exposure to problematic and illegal content as well as harassment and bullying. These risks are not confined to their local areas but occur all around the world. Parents and teachers do not have direct experience with the risks posed by new-media technologies. Addressing the risks, that occur online carries different challenges and requires broader collaboration to find innovative solutions.

Technological Development and Child Abuse

Technological development in the field of information and introduction of computers has made a significant turning point in the history of human civilization. It has brought about a sea change in all fields of human activity. It has resulted in enhanced efficiency. Productivity and quality of outputs are in every walk of life. The new developments are posing challenges to the fundamental principles of law that worked well before the advent of this technology. It is a fact that it has been misused in every sphere and every corner of this rem. Misuse and abuse play a vital role to fulfil the tendency and work of criminals in the cyberspace.

New multimedia technology is being misused and abused by the criminals in cyberspace. Cyber pornography, online child pornography, cyber spamming, cyber hacking, cyber fraud, cyber terrorism, flowing of warm and virus etc., are cyber crimes. These are increasingly proliferating at a lightning speed in the age of information technology revolution. Cyber crime differs from traditional crimes, crimes against women and girls are increasing on cyber space. Many children are victimized without their knowledge about cyberspace.[38] Cyber crimes are carried out in a variety of circumstance and in a sophisticated form. Cyber crimes are harmful computer generated acts committed from or against a computer or not net work are different from other crime. The crimes are easy to learn as to how to connect, the world without physical presence. In these days organized crimes and cyber crimes are begin to overlapping the system. Internet is a means to exploitation for fulfilling their goal in an organized manner. Cyber crimes are now are one of the most complex international and global problems. Empirical surveys (If any) have all stated that a majority of the victims of cyber stalking are women and girl. The present criminal justice is inept in protecting victims and adequately criminalizing the act of cyber stalking in the country.[39]

Child pornography in cyber space is not only a national but also an international legal challenge. It need intensive study, research and worldwide awareness to protect minors from computer system network compact disk, (C.D) (D.V.D), video and other information processing devices which are easily accessible to children in contemporary social environment. Freedom of speech and expression and right to information constitute the bed rock of a democratic polity prior to the spectacular growth of new multimedia technology. But it is interest and new communication convergence technology which can connect many people with any other people at one and the same time. Worldwide only one mobile phone with facilities can act as television, telephone tape recorder fax machine camera video, World Wide Web and Internet system etc. The younger generation has a craze for this new technology but most of the times they are unaware about the result of misuse and abuse of it.

This problem has been compounded much more by the introduction of Internet. Internet has offered tremendous information incentives to all and sundry in all walks of life online service can now be substituted for newspapers radio, television and telephone. This means services such as paperless communication evaluated in terms of constant benefit is also matchless and as it reduces the expense of physical elements of other media, for their distribution and display is the need of hour in the modern arena. In these days the world became a village and one could be able to gain all type of information. In the criminal consequences of computer related conducts children are the most vulnerable victims as they go through visualizing the mass of materials and get confused. Incidentally the Cyberspace is the environment with which a computer hacker operates passes the abusive scenes to the kids. In some cases the operator are identified or may not be identified but in gradual process internet became a common source of sexual and sensual entertainment for all including children.[40] Cyber stalking, online booming, disseminating indecent materials to minors, sexual performance by a child, repeated and threatening behaviours and consequential off-line harassment are few computer related problems that haunt children. The user may find it in the form of demand through web cameras. The reason for such hacking by young children may be due to fact finding. Contact with stranger or opposite sex of such age group children will use comfortably that site of electronic media in order to meet their gratification and curiosity of desire. The possible cause is pornographic activity stalker activity where it is most likelihood of children being victim. In most of the cases the service areas are in the nature of Kids area and are identified as Teens BB, Games BB and Chat to which a computer user makes contact with the other side through e-mail; may be friend with and extract personal information and in gradual process may transmit mail containing sex information, shyness and respectability in the society force them to remain as innocent victims. Communication has become speedy and easy in contemporary society. Criminals and offenders use the devices to fulfil all sort of their objects in aid of all scope and facilities of communication.

In recent times the cyber spaces has become a fertile field for illegal activity and often lead to violent crimes. To combat the same, India has passed an information technology act, 2000. Law enacted to serve the needs of the society. It has to keep pace with the aspirations and need of the society as well as to take into consideration the changing concept of the value. It is only with an intention to serve the social purpose and serve the society and to protect the victims from the sorrow and danger. Now-a-days spamming multimedia service-video and still pornographic clip and there by child on line pornography are increasing day by day in India like other countries but only possession of pornographic materials is not a crime under section 67 of the Information Technology Act, 2000. It is alarming to discover what type of pornography is being generated on the internet and the Information Technology Act is capable to protect the common practice of today's pornographer. As such only one provision under section 75 only need reasonable link to computer activities, which is relevant to jurisdictional issues only. Out of this there is no such remarkable provision which keeps an eye on the offenders activities, as such ample of cases are real cyber shock and shaken the momentum about the tragedy exposed in popular networking site Myspace.com which was involved in a series cases and Bazee.com having fun with girl on 24th November 2004.

Most recent development is that, through the video clips, SMS, MMS of child sexual abuse clippings are spread all around the nook corner of the world with in a pulse of time. Those clippings are downloaded and sold on roadside betel shops. It is quite unfortunate to elaborate here that the future of nation is sold in road side as an instrument of amusement.[41]

Especially in the era of communication convergence where cyber crimes are increasing day by day, where cyber crimes are increasing, it is our prime duty to adopt certain measures to prevent and control child pornography in cyber space. These measures are stated below:

There is need to adopt a uniform legal system worldwide because this is not only a national problem but also an International problem. The Information Act 2000 does not contain specific provisions on child pornography and therefore it needs a refused law and make special provisions for the protection in every sphere of the scene. Investigation of cyber crime is difficult no doubt but with the help of experts difficult problems can be solved. In future we require more number of such investigation stations in different parts of location to check the cyber crime.

Children and Crime

Crime is a social and economic phenomenon in a human society. It has been with us in varying degrees since time immemorial. Crime is a legal concept and has a sentence of law. Crime against children, child abuse and neglect are increased with the passage of time, the change in social conditions and mores, emergence of new crimes and progress in science and Technology paved a root for organized crimes. The UNICEF's flagship publication report was released as 'The State of the World's Children 2011'. The State of the World's Children report 'Adolescence: An Age of Opportunity' is pure theory of the subject. In his address Governor of Orissa, Murlidhar Chandrakant Bhandare expressed that, an estimated 7.9 million adolescents representing over 19 per cent of the State's population living here. The vast majority of these adolescents, 6.7 million, live in rural areas. And they are the ones, who hold the key to State's social and economic progress.[42] Social and economical causes have impact on crime causation. Despite daily attention in crime in the news paper television reports and radio awareness programme. It is surprising for everybody about its exposures, and its impact on society. The occurrence of crime is not only increasing in figures but also in respect too of its gravity. Crime and sensation of crime cause wide-spread alarm and now it is a major concern for the people of the society. Crime gives an absolute picture of the crime as well as juvenile offender situation in the every sphere. Juvenile delinquency refers to the antisocial or criminal activity of the child (below 18 years of age for boys and girls). In true context the age of child has been defined to be below 18 years as per Juvenile Justice Act, 2000. The criminal behaviour and action of a child exposes when he commits an offence. For the purpose of this profile project a total of 24,201 cases of crimes against Children were reported in the country during 2009 as compared to 22,500 cases during 2008, suggesting an increase of 7.6 per cent. Among IPC crimes, number of Foeticide cases increased from 73 in 2008 to 123 in 2009, registering an increase of 68.5 per cent over 2008. Highest incidences of cases were reported about the organized crimes by N.C.R.B. The tiny aged children legitimate and ill-legitimate are controlled by prostitutes. Prostitution is an organized crime, where the children serve as a ready market for stolen merchandise thus compounding the total crime picture. The sale and use of narcotics and drugs gravitate to the high earnings of prostitutes. The girl child is deployed for blackmailing and extortion is common by products of the profession, Prostitution attracts the easy money with the help of the 'criminals' who are below the age of 18 years.

It has been noted that theft and robbery add to a major percentage of these crimes. Murder, rape, dacoity, burglary, kidnapping are a few more that add to the rest of it. On the basis of the available statistics, an inference can be drawn that these crimes are on the increasing path. The abuses of children are caused to be seen as a serious social stigma. Both primary and secondary sources reflect that children more than 75 per cent are abandoned, destitute and their age group is between 12-18 years and 35 per cent out of this belonging to the backward class and migrated offenders living in the streets of the slum area. Economic motive seems to be the main motivating factor for committing crime.[43] An important fact is that in order to gain economically they committed the crime knowing all the consequences well. Females and girls are also not deviant from this subject. Female crimes are the product of chain of circumstances as poverty, illiteracy and hobby to do this for easy access of money. Frustration coupled with illegitimate opportunity structure lead to crime. The abuse could also be invisible in many forms, but the offences were construed as Crimes and the author tries to amplify the children's concern. Much more research still needs to be done in this issue.

Aforesaid analysis data and comparative figures over a period of time indicate an increase or decrease in the incidence of crime requiring appropriate crime control movement to stop the menace. It is a question in mind, where is the voice in criminal justice system to save the interests of victims which suffered a lot and could not get justice due to regular court procedures, It is often believed that a victim has zero play in crime and the entire legal system supports the accused. As a result the accused has much scope for acquittal.

There is no separate classification of offences against children. Generally, the offences committed against children or the crimes in which children are the victims are considered as crime against children. It is important to acknowledge that the concept of victimization is complex, multidimensional, and even problematic. There is an infinite array of situation or circumstances that can lead to victimization. The various crimes that are being registered and investigated by different law enforcement agencies were broadly grouped under the following categories for statistical information system. Broad classification of crimes under the Indian Penal Code[44] such as; Child Rape, Kidnapping and Abduction of Children, Procreation of minor girls, Selling/Buying of girls for Prostitution, Abetment to Suicide etc. Crime against children includes violation under certain sections of Indian Penal Code and Special and Local Laws. Legal perspectives like Indian penal code and the various protective and preventive 'Special and Local Laws' specifically mention the offences, wherein children are victims. The objects of I.P.C seem to be frustrating in the present Indian context. In state the crime scenario is distressing. The performances of the system and its engrained loop holes have paved the way for the criminals to make a mockery of criminal law. The common people are losing faith on criminal justices system.[45]

The amendments, notifications and enactments should be implemented in such a manner as a result of which the goal can be achieved. As an observation, many studies pointed out that no child is ever born criminal. No research studies and findings have been able to clearly establish a casual relationship between genetic endowment of a child and future criminality. The social, economic and other factors which have been the root causes of Juvenile Delinquency need to deal with at the very initial stage. Every society must, therefore, devote full attention to ensure that children are properly cared for and brought up in a proper atmosphere, where they could receive adequate training, education and guidance in order that they may be able to have their rightful place in the society when they grown up.

In recent years, children and their problems have been receiving attention of both government and the society. Children need and have the right to all the support as the future citizens of the country. But it has been seen that the problems are enormous and never ending, thus resulting in lack of everything that has been done till today. If these problems are not curbed soon then the growth of the children will be hampered giving a dark future to our country.

FOOTNOTES

1. Rights and Opportunities: The Situation of Children and Women in India, UNICEF, 1998, p. 7.
2. Situational Analysis of Children in India: North Centre of SCF: Rajasthan and Uttar Pradesh, Save the Children Fund, 2000, p. 2.
3. The State of the Worlds Children, Unicef Report, 2000, p. 13.
4. Jyothi Mehera, "Impact of HIV/AIDS on Children in Manipur: Rapid Assessment Study", Manipur State AIDS Control Society, 2001. pp. 79-84.
5. Pinki Virani, Bitter Chocolate – Child Sexual Abuse in India, Penguin Books India, 2000, p. 12.
6. Annual Report, 1999-2000, Department of Women and Child Development, Ministry of Human Resource Development, pp. 56-57.
7. Study Report on Sexual Abuse of Children in India, National Commission for Women, 2001, p. 67.
8. Statistics on Children in India (Hand-book), (1989-99), National Institute of Public Co-operation and Child Development, Government of India.
9. Lakshmi Dhar Mishra, Child Labour in India, Oxford University Press, New Delhi, 2000, p. 67.
10. *Ibid*. p. 69.
11 Helen Sekarm Child Labour Legislation in India – A Study in Retrospect and Prospect, V. V. Giri National Labour Institute, New Delhi, 1997, p. 71.
12. Jyoti Mehra, "Reducing Risk Behaviour Related to HIV/AIDS and Drug Abuse Among Street Children", National Report, Ministry of Welfare, UNDCP, WHO and NACO, 1996, p. 37.
13. Study on Child Abuse, 2007, Ministry of Women and Child Development, GOI, p. 19.

14. Uma A. Sehgal, "Child Abuse in India: A Theoretical Overview", *Indian Journal of Social Work*, Vol. 52, July 1991, pp. 162.
15. Subhash Singh, "Growing Problem of Child Abuse and Neglect", *Criminal Law Journal*, Vol. 100, September 1994, pp. 81-88.
16. Report on National Seminar on Implementation of Child Labour Projects, National Resource Centre on Child Labour, V. V. Giri National Labour Institute, New Delhi, 1997.
17. S. N. Behera, Socio-economic Dimensions of Child Labour – Issues and Policy Options, Discovery Publishing House, New Delhi, 1996, p. 76.
18. Award Digest: *Journal of Labour Legislation*, National Labour Institute, New Delhi, 2002.
19. Education for All – Early Childhood Care and Education, NIEPA, GOI, 2000.
20. The Indian Express, May 15, 1997.
21. Rameshwari Devi and Ravi Prakash, Social Work Practice, Mangal Deep Publications, Jaipur, 2001, p. 42.
22. Annual Report, CACL, 2001, p. 19.
23. *Ibid*.
24. S. Kusuma Kumari, 'Abolition of Child Labour: Chasing a Mirage or Reality', *Supreme Court Journal*, Vol. 25, June, 2007, pp. 42-48.
25. Mohd. Ishaque Qureshi, "Child Exploitation: Violation of Human Rights", *Aligarh Law Journal*, Vol. XIII, 1998, p. 34.
26. K. Srinivasan and Chander Shekhar, "Reviewing Reproductive and Child Health Programmes in India", *Economic and Political Weekly*, Vol. 42, July 2007, p. 27-28.
27. Mahesh Koolwal, "Illegitimate Child vis-à-vis Human Rights", *Journal of Human Rights*, Vol. 38, 2008, p. 207-213.
28. The Dharitri, March 15, 2002.
29. Naveen Souda, "Child Labour in India", *Andhra Law Times*, October 2007, pp. 21-23.
30. Ravinder Kaur Pasricha, "Violation of Child Rights and Victimization of Child Labourers: Working in Restaurants and Dhabas", *Indian Journal of Criminology and Criminalistics*, Sept-Dec., 2007, pp. 56-63.
31. D. Rufus, "Child Abuse: An Overview", *Indian Police Journal*, Vol. 56, Jan-March, 2009, pp. 28-37.
32. Annual Report, NCRB, 2009, pp. 56-57.
33. The Times of India, April 14, 2007, p. 4.

34. Jyoti Mehra, "Reducing Risk Behaviour Related to HIV/AIDS and Drug Abuse Among Street Children", National Report, Ministry of Welfare, UNDCP, WHO and NACO, 1996, p. 39.
35. Kamaljeet Singh and Harish Verma, "Growing Child Sex Tourism in Third-World Countries: An Overview", *Civil and Military Law Journal,* Vol. 43, July-December, 2007, pp. 114-18.
36. The New Indian Express, July 23, 2007, p. 3.
37. Valsamma Paul, "Sexual Abuse of Children – Need for Legislation", *Indian Bar Review,* Vol. 32, (1 and 2), 2005, p. 114.
38. Raghunath Patnaik, "Vulnerability of Children through Cyber Crimes", *Indian Bar Review,* Vol. XXX, No. 2 and 3, 2003, p. 405.409.
39. *Ibid.*
40. S.C. Agarwal, "Computer Ethics, Child Sexual Abuse, Pornography and the Regulation of Child Pornography on the Internet", CBI Bulletin, Vol. 10, January 2002, pp. 7-11.
41. *Ibid.*
42. The Samaj, Bhubaneswar, May 11, 2011, p. 2.
43. S.B.N. Prakash, "Criminal Justice System and Juvenile or Child in Conflict with Law", *Karnataka Law Journal,* Vol. 15, 2009, pp. 9-24.
44. The Indian Penal Code, 1860, Section 354/375/376/377.
45. Ashok Tiwary, "Child Care: Socio-Legal Measures", *Indian Journal of Criminology and Criminalistics,* Vol. 28 (1), Jan-April, 2007, pp. 11-19.

5 Prevention and Rehabilitation

At the dawn of the 21st century human life is an experienced uncertainties and mounting stresses, which are un-denied and inevitable in every spheres of life. Man is born in a family and dies in a family in a given society. Family nourishes, educates, protects and shapes the destiny of its members. Children were considered as a pool of human potentials, on which the destiny of a nation depends. Children are considered as the Gift of God. Yes, god has created human beings as equal without any discrimination as to their skill power, will power, grasping power, intellectual power, etc. But it is the human beings who discriminate; misuse, abuse the mankind and treat them as an object. In fact the fault lies only on the selfish nature of the human being. Child is like a flower, childhood is a golden period. It is the birth right of a child to enjoy the love of parents, neighbours and society at large. Families and children themselves need to understand the rights and together create an enabling environment, where in a child is protected from abuse and exploitation. Today's world requires to focus on economic and social policies that address poverty, income gaps, unemployment, urban overcrowding, gender and other forms of inequality and other environmental factors that undermine society. States should ensure those children's rights which are disseminated and understood, including the children. The primary responsibility of protecting children from abuse and neglect lies with the families or the primary caregivers. However, communities and civil society and all other person are also responsible for the care and protection of children. The overarching responsibility is that of the State and it is the State that has to create a protective environment and provide a safety net for children, who fall into vulnerable and exploitative situations. The society, like a family must provide for the basic needs of children, as a first priority for its own survival and development. Child abuse prevention must be oriented by the satisfaction of the child's needs in their socio-cultural context, which are always based on a thorough knowledge of the variable aspects too. The vulnerability of children abuse is linked to their age and evolving capacity. Some children because of gender, race, ethnic origin, disability or social status are particularly vulnerable. Due to ignorance of right to express their views children are not given proper weight. They are also part of the society and having equal right to every thing. It is important to emphasise that the rights of children, with specific reference to basic rights to health, nutrition, education, shelter and protection from exploitation should be enforced most stringently because they are children, irrespective of where they came from and where they have to go. But one thing is crystal clear how to bring them to main stream of the society. Various categories of children face many problem and challenges, when they are out of home. They are mainly street children, working children, deprived children, and children in conflict with law.

The problem of child exploitation is grave and how to check this problem is on important factor. The nation should be conscious about the well-being of the child. National policy for the welfare of children should be framed and implemented so as the feature of citizens may grown to be physically fit, mentally alert and morally healthy to do best. Their entitlements and rights flow from the fact that they are citizens of this nation. The centre and State beings have the obligation to fulfil the same. Today there is a very different approach to the child. It is accepted in principle that the child has the right to state and his or her opinion should be properly considered in decisions concerning the child.

Prevention of abuse against children is like any other prevention of crime in the scenario. The momentum needs to be sustained and should be carried forward in the form of a movement that will take responsibility by all civilized personas of this society. The road to sustainable development and creation of a protective environment for Children is the right of children. Children are protected under the UN Convention on the Rights of the Child (CRC). The CRC provides an incentive to expand the scope of fundamental rights by Constitutional amendments and/or interpretations of the law. As per the Indian Constitution, Articles 14, 21 and 21A, the Indian State is obligated to secure basic rights for children as citizens of India, displaced or otherwise. Article 12 of the Convention on the Rights of the Child elaborate about children's right to express their views freely on all matters that affect them and to have those views given due weight. Children's own views and experiences must contribute to prevention and other interventions to stop abuse against them. Children – acting voluntarily and with appropriate ethical safeguards – can make a significant contribution to both describing the problem of violence against them, and also to the design of services and other interventions that they can trust and use. The obligation to ascertain and take children's views seriously must be built into the legal framework for child protection. A reduction of gender based violence against children cannot be expected unless prohibitive sanctions are combined with socio-economic policies that encourage responsible parenting for all children.

There are various categories of children who face many problems when they are out of home. Children should not be exploited in any manner being the future of a nation. Exploitation abridges development of children. Exploitation of children shall be prevented in order to guarantee their development. Children belonging to minority group shall be ensured of their rights to practice his culture, religion and language in this rem. It shall be the duty of the State to ensure protection of the child from all forms of exploitation. This has not been proposed with a view to encourage such activity but because believing criminalization is a harsh measure intended to impose a skewed conception of morality on children, when more rational solution lies in counseling and treatment. It is pointed out that the problems are associated with treating the offence of grooming as a crime. Finally, it is urged that thesis is a need for a provision for anonymity of child victims in cases of sexual abuse because disclosure of their identity may have the negative impact of leaving a mark of indelible trauma on their sensitive minds and dissuading such victims from pursuing the course of criminal justice. In every society, more particularly in our country, there is a vast difference between the law in books and the law in action; this is so because of rapidly changing social realities and change in social behaviour. It is an urgent need to strengthen and integrate their strategies and measures for reducing the number of vulnerable children. The focus should be on conspicuous flow in the criminal justice system that is responsible for justices. Miscarriage of justices' delay in bringing cases to try, allegations of bias contributed to an erosion of public confidence in a criminal justices system. In every system including juvenile justice there are certain methods which have been adopted for the prevention and prohibition. Juveniles do not come into contact with hardened criminals and their chances of reformation are not blighted by contact with criminal offenders. Many measures are adopted for the correction of delinquents. It is pointed out that fairly well defined delinquents are differentiated in much ways-in accordance to the offences, but it requires different treatment for different types of delinquencies. In this juvenile justice system a pronged approach is made to it that is: *(i)* corrective *(ii)* preventative, and both the processed are valuable and applicable in every respect to check the malice.

The rehabilitation of juvenile differs in several ways from the rehabilitation of adult criminals. Because of their young age, they have not been crystallized with discouraging finality and thus they are amenable to treatment and counselling. Basically there are two forms of treatment programmes for juvenile delinquency that is preventive and rehabilitative programme. How ever, it is an evergreen practice that child has been victimized in every sphere in the nook corner of the society. The legal provisions, that are designed to protect children from economic exploitation, cannot be enforced in most cases, since relevant administrative, economic and social measures have not been taken. At the same time, it offers special protection to the rights of children. Therefore, children's human rights are very much guaranteed under the international law. There is an obligation to respect the dignity, self reliance of the physically or mentally disabled child. For the sake of rehabilitation of children the rehabilitation Council of India Act came into force in the year 1992. The noble aspects of the Act purports and covers about the human resources development in the areas of disabilities, the major objectives of disability rehabilitations are: *(a)* Regulate human resource development in rehabilitation throughout the country; *(b)* Certify qualified personnel and professionals in the field of disabilities; *(c)* Ensure quality, standard and uniformity in the rehabilitation programmes offered throughout the country. Therefore the Human resource development programmes ranging from training at grass root level of India, but it's quite unfortunate to elaborate the same that the disability children are the victims in every respect to achieve the objects. The research work offers solutions to ameliorate the sufferings of the juvenile community as thought by such various categories of people as sociologists, social workers, legislators, administrators, and the judiciary decisions. As such new communication systems and digital technology have made dramatic changes in the way we live, to prevent the possible misuse arising out of transactions and other dealings concluded over the electronic medium, it is also proposed to sort out the consequences of alternative course of action.

A careful work is necessary for the effectiveness of prevention. At first stage, the creation of an environment where in discussion on child abuse has been initiated, to develop strength and implement national laws to establish the criminal responsibility of service providers, customers and intermediaries on child prostitution, child trafficking, child pornography and other unlawful sexual activity. In recent days the media has started highlighting such issues and an understanding of their gravity is gaining momentum. This understanding must be translated into action, not only by the central government, but also state governments and civil society. In the case of sex tourism, it is necessary to for strengthen and implement the law to stop the acts committed by overseas visitors against children. There is need to strengthen or establish networks between national and international law enforcement authorities to monitor the commercial sexual exploitation of children to check the practice.

This empirical study has established beyond doubt that child abuse exists in India and the incidence is much higher than generally perceived. While the situation is alarming, it is important to take cognizance of the fact that the study was not done with the intention of creating fear and alarm but to high light valuable factors responsible for the child abuse to do best in all. The prevention of child abuse is almost universally proclaimed to be an important social policy. Prevention of abuse can be achieved in a number of ways and indifferent contexts. That framework consists of three levels of services: a comprehensive system of care for improving outcomes for children and families need to include strategies that co-ordinate resources across the entire continuum, from primary to secondary and also to tertiary prevention. Some basic principles and practices of child prevention are enumerated below:

Measures to Abuse Prevention

1. *Best Interest of a Child:* The best interest and well-being of the Child shall be the paramount consideration at every society in every stage of childhood. This principle seeks about to ensure the physical, emotional, intellectual, social

and moral development of the child so as to make the child a useful and good citizen by ameliorating the impediments to the healthy development of the child through proper utilisation of health and education policy. Natural parents are the fore most consideration for care taker/adoption of child, if the problem arose regarding care and protection then court should appoint a guardian as a care taker to care and protect the child and his interest.

2. *Protection of a Child:* The State, duty bearers and every person shall take every possible measure to protect and support a child from all forms of physical or mental violence, injury, abuse, neglect, maltreatment or exploitation including sexual assault and exposure of children to psychological stress through reality shows and competitions, through effective procedures and programmes, as well as for identification, reporting, referral, investigation and treatment for judicial involvement.
3. *Equality and Non-discrimination – 'Leave no Child behind':* Equality of access and opportunity for all has to be guaranteed to every Child and there shall be no discrimination on the basis of age, sex, place of birth, disability, race, ethnicity, socio-economic status, caste, cultural practices, work, activity and behaviour of the Child or that of the parents or Guardians of the child or any other consideration.
4. *Individuality and Participation:* The Child shall be respected and treated as an individual capable of forming and expressing ideas and opinions. According to the age of child (must not be below 7 years) the opinion of the Child shall be sought and considered, regarding the welfare of the child.
5. *Privacy and Confidentiality:* The Child's rights to privacy and confidentiality shall be protected by all means and through all stages of the proceedings.
6. *Non-Stigmatizing Language, Decisions and Actions:* Non-stigmatizing language must be strictly adhered to, and the use of adverse or accusatory words shall be prohibited.

7. *Avoidance of Harm*: At all stages from initial contact with the Child until final disposal of the case, extreme care shall be taken to avoid any harm to the well-being and safety of the Child. All duty bearers must consider these cases to be a priority and utilise the maximum of the available resources to ensure that the Child is provided justice promptly and is eventually rehabilitated back into society.
8. *Non-criminalization of a Child*: At all stages of the proceedings, the child shall not be criminalized, as the child is the victim upon whom the offence has been committed. Capacity building programme of all those who work with and for the children must be developed to contribute to eliminate all form of violence against them. States conduct programmes both for professionals and non-professionals, who work with or for children and families to prevent, detect and respond to violence against children. Codes of conduct and rules and regulation for standard practice and implementation should be formulated, implemented and incorporated for prohibition and rejection of all forms of violence. Working to prevent child abuse and neglect has borrowed other disciplines, including public health, education, and mental health, to influence and guide practice. That framework consists of three levels of services: *(a) Primary* prevention programmes, directed at the general population (universal); *(b) Secondary* prevention programmes, targeted to individuals or families in which maltreatment is more likely (high risk); and *(c) Tertiary* prevention programmes, targeted toward families in which abuse has already occurred (indicated) which are described as follows:
   (a) Primary Prevention: Primary prevention activities are directed at the general population and attempt to stop maltreatment before it occurs. All members of the community have access to and may benefit from these services. Primary prevention activities with a universal focus seek to raise the awareness of the general public, service providers, and decision-makers about the scope

and problems associated with child maltreatment. Universal approaches to primary prevention might include: *(i)* Public service announcements that encourage positive parenting. *(ii)* Parent education programmes and support groups that focus on child development. *(iii)* Age-appropriate expectations, and the roles and responsibilities of parenting. *(iv)* Family support and family strength programmes that enhance the ability of families to access existing services, and resources to support positive interactions among family members. *(v)* Public awareness campaigns that provide information on how and where to report suspected child abuse and neglect.

(b) *Secondary Prevention:* Secondary prevention activities with a high-risk focus are offered to populations that have one or more risk factors associated with child maltreatment, such as poverty, parental substance abuse, young parental age, parental mental health concerns, and parental or child disabilities. Programmes may target services for communities or neighbourhoods that have a high incidence of any or all of these risk factors. Approaches to prevention programmes that focus on high-risk populations might include:

Parent education programmes located in high schools, focusing on teen parents, or those within substance abuse treatment programmes for mothers and families with young children. Parent support groups that help parents deal with their everyday stresses and meet the challenges and responsibilities of parenting. Home visiting programmes that provide support and assistance to expecting and new mothers in their homes. Respite care for families that have children with special needs. Family resource centres that offer information and referral services to families living in low-income neighbourhoods.

(c) *Tertiary Prevention:* Tertiary prevention activities focus on families where maltreatment has already occurred

(indicated) and seek to reduce the negative consequences of the maltreatment and to prevent its recurrence. These prevention programmes may include services such as: Intensive family preservation services with trained mental health counsellors that are available to families 24 hours per day for a short period of time (*e.g.*, 6 to 8 weeks). Parent mentor programmes with stable, non-abusive families acting as 'role models' and providing support to families in crisis. Parent support groups that help parents transform negative practices and beliefs into positive parenting behaviours and attitudes, mental health services for children and families affected by maltreatment to improve family communication and functioning. Without describing the aspects of ecological prevention, it is fruitless to complete the prevention framework; therefore it is outlined below as a last resort for prevention strategy.

Ecological Framework of Prevention

An ecological framework for prevention is based on the following assumptions: Children and families exist as part of an ecological system. This means that prevention strategies must target interventions at multiple levels: the individual, the family, the community, and society. Primary responsibility for the development and well-being of children lies within the family, and all segments of society must support families as they raise their children. Assuring the well-being of all families is the cornerstone of a healthy society and requires universal access to support programmes and services.

Prevention is better than cure, which may not be realised but it is a fact indeed. Child abuse is a growing issue in every time; it remains a strongly entrenched problem. As such variety of interventions could prevent violence specifically on violence against children inside the family or outside, by implementation of laws, policies and programmes, that strengthen families and community. Health is the greatest wealth of a human being; so health services for reproductive and maternal and child health are the first line of action to reduce neglect and abuse against children from their earliest moments of life. Children should receive more protection while compared with adults and no impunity for those who perpetrate violence against children, but care must be taken to ensure that child victims do not suffer further through insensitive enforcement of the law. Prosecutions and formal interventions, in particular within the family, should occur when necessary to protect a child from significant harm and when judged it should be in favour of the best interests of the child. There are many factors which are supplemented by additional recommendations for specific abuse happened in home and family, schools, care and justice systems, places where children are working legally or illegally, and the community at large with duty and obligation.

Preventative Measures

As parents, they should always know where their child is, what he or she is doing and with whom. Unfortunately, it is virtually impossible to ensure that child will never be a victim of sexual abuse. However, there are certain preventive measures that can and should be taken to reduce the odds of the child experiencing this trauma.

Preventative measures could include:

- Encouraging your child to talk to you about what they have been doing each day, including time spent with others.
- Create an atmosphere in which the child feels free to talk about any problems with parents.
- Explain and discuss sexual abuse with the child openly and encourage questions.
- Explain to the child that their body belongs to them alone.
- Encourage the children to say 'No' when they believe their rights are being infringed upon.
- Make clear the difference between abusive touching and acceptable demonstrations of affection by family or friends.

- Assure the children that parents want to know if someone tries to touch them, whether it is a stranger or someone in the family.
- Instruct the child to avoid being unaccompanied in potentially dangerous places such as deserted areas (bush land, parking lots, etc.,) and public toilets.
- Always encourage children to travel with a friend, rather than alone.
- The parents must ensure to the point of dropping and picking children up from meeting points.
- Discussions with the child regarding sexual abuse should be carried out in an open manner which does not frighten the child to the point of being hesitant to engage in normal social activities.
- Child abuse should be included in the context of behaviour by others which the child can discuss openly with you. It is, however, imperative that the importance of these precautionary procedures be clearly understood by the child.

Prevention Programmes

Standards for prevention programmes, research on what works, information on the role of related professionals, and resources for specific types of programmes are to be found. Find standards for prevention programmes, reports from State programmes, and information on types of programmes addressing the prevention of child abuse and neglect. Civil society and Government should club their hands to strive out transform attitudes that normalize abuse against children a positive and non-abusive environments must be created for and with children in their homes, schools, other institutions and communities, stereotypical gender roles and discrimination, acceptance of corporal punishment, and the harmful traditional practices including public and parent education, advocacy campaigns and training standards, Reports from State programme, Home visiting, Early childhood programmes, Parent education, Parent support groups, Respite and crisis care, Family resource centres, preventing abusive head trauma, preventing sexual abuse. Preventing the recurrence of abuse and neglect, Programmes for families affected by domestic violence, Programmes for families affected by substance abuse, Children must invariably be listened to and taken seriously. From the year 2004 child line exposes different type of cases which has been reporting regularly. So States should use national resources to collect proper data for compiling and analysing for dissemination to monitor progress from time to time. So data should be collected from village to urban place, according to birth, death and marriage and all data registries with full national coverage should be created and maintained. Further States should also create and maintain data on children without parental care and on children in the criminal justice system. Data should be disaggregated by sex, age, urban/rural, household and family characteristics, education and ethnicity. It should also be incorporated into a national research agenda on violence against children across settings, where violence occurs, including through interview studies with children and parents, with particular attention to vulnerable groups of girls and boys.

The development of a national research agenda on violence against children across settings is critical for knowledge building and improved programme development. Such plans should include children, parents, service providers and others, and use a range of methods such as interview studies, improved reporting and registration systems and investigation procedures, and regular surveys, with particular attention given to vulnerable groups of girls and boys. No country can be complacent about violence against children and more research into prevalence, causes, and prevention is needed everywhere. Our ability to determine the magnitude, characteristics, and trends of many forms of violence against children is poor, even in industrialized countries. All countries must increase their capacity to monitor deaths, injuries and behaviours associated with violence against children to determine whether the problem is getting better or worse, and the association between these trends and various strategies for prevention.

Prevention, Rehabilitation and Treatment

Prevention is better if the problem is worse but rehabilitation and treatment are concerned which provide the curative methods for the future problems. Generally the rehabilitation and treatment are inter-disciplinary in nature and it can be implemented by both the means that is individual and group level. The institutional and non-institutional activities are right bases to implement properly for the benefit of the society. Adoption is another non-institutional measure, which restores family care for the children who are deprived of their real family life. Adopted child gets all the rights in the same way as that of natural child would get. In fact adoption provides a name, a legal status and permanent family to the child. Rehabilitation is often a long process, but informal or formal psycho-social support may be helpful. Drop-in centres can provide a non-threatening environment where children can choose to come and go as they please. Drama and art activities can also be used to work through trauma caused by abuse. Residential care should only be a last resort but temporary care may be beneficial. These approaches are as follows:

- Adopt non-punitive approach to child victims, taking particular care that judicial procedures do not aggravate the trauma the child has already experienced.
- Provide social, medical and psychological counselling, and other support to child victims and their families.
- Train medical personnel, teacher's social workers, NGOs and others working to help child victims; and Promote alternative means of livelihood, where appropriate, with adequate support services for child victims and their families.

There has been significant development in the area of disability rehabilitation since then. However, considering the nature of the condition, it is essential to see what has been the value addition in the area of intellectual disabilities (mental retardation) and what more needs to be done. The current status of person's with mental retardation in various stages of their lives range from infancy to adulthood. The other factors are adoption and psychological counseling, vocational training and awareness campaign which play a vital role in every aspect. Punitive and non-punitive approach to child victims of sexual exploitation, provide social, medical, and other supports to child victims and their families, facilitate the recovery and reintegration of child victims in their communities and families and where institutionalization of the child is necessary, ensure that it is for the shortest period possible in accordance with the child's best interests to promote alternative means of livelihood for survival and to rehabilitation in the main streams of the society which is the need of hour.

Prevention and early detection of disabilities, education, employment, economic rehabilitation, community empowerment and community based rehabilitation have all been given priority by the Government through various schemes and also support to non-government organizations. The government is shifting his responsibility of work and welfare means by providing various aids to the N.G.Os. The individual and family based programmes are progressive but not satisfactory. It is essential to create a safe and secure environment for runaway children picked from railway platforms to shelter homes, government homes, institutions and other NGO shelters, to protect the child form neglect and abuse, to reunite the runaway or separated child with family, and address the causes that had caused the child to run away to prevent them from running away again, as the family in the best place for a child. Track and reunite children for a limited period of time to assess and encourage their integration with the family. Facilitate the child protection system from the grassroots to national level with a view to rehabilitate children with their families. Generate and share practice-based knowledge related to runaway and separated children, within the child protection system, so as to improve interventions in the interest of rehabilitating the child with family. Implement the best practices related to quality rehabilitation of children with their families, and to facilitate the implementation of these practices by the State and NGO sector working on the issue of runaway and separated children. Facilitate the engagement of civil society with the state on issues related to runaway and separated children. It is to bring to limelight that there are various schemes of sponsorship of children such as individual-to individual sponsorship, group sponsorship or community sponsorship. It is also another non-institutional measure which is being recognised and available as alternative to institutional care of children. The institutional measures cannot be overlooked due to many disadvantages but it has to be used as a last resort for the welfare of children.

The working children are identified through child labour survey, withdrawn from work and put into the special schools, so as to provide them with enabling environment to join mainstream education system. In these Special Schools, besides formal education, they are provided stipend of Rs. 1000/- per month, nutrition, vocational training and regular health check ups. In addition, efforts are also made to target the families of these children, so as to cover them under various developmental and income/employment generation programmes of the Government. The scheme also envisages awareness generation campaigns against the evils of child labour and enforcement of child labour laws. The Labour Department should assist children who have completed Class X to get vocational training by linking them up to local ITIs, NGO run vocational training programmes and private sector initiatives. They should not run vocational training centres as the track record of vocational training centres set up by the labour departments is extremely poor. The labour department should instead help older children to get placements in the job market. Youth volunteers, gram panchayats, school teachers, officers of labour department and so on must all be given training about child labour and their respective roles in abolition of child labour.

Family Programmes

It is bitter truth that without the basic need mankind can't survive in the society. Basic need, in case of the child is personal and psychological needs essential for their proper development. As a human being, food, clothing, shelter, and health are the basic needs of life and sustenance. Any other basic needs are the quality of life, which is meaningless without health which has direct linkage with diet. Unless persons get the minimum food to survive today, there will no future tomorrow to enjoy the fountain of life. Our focus is on the availability of regular meal, breakfast and Tiffin, the intake of protein and vitamin, and the level of nourishment. Clothing and shelter are the important basic items of a human being for which he is struggling ever since. It seems from the various reports that homelessness is a growing problem for children, its rise has been attributed to many factors but interdisciplinary in nature. The food, clothing and shelter are related to each other and all the three affect the health. It is the ripen moment to examine and analyse the actual situation about the facilities of health. The proper health of human beings hinges on the combined effect of three distinct, yet intimately related, aspects of health services-curative, preventive and promotive, therefore to highlight the aspects of health about children is essential in every proportions.

Family is one of important social institutions and plays a significant role in the care and development of children. Every family is expected to provide all opportunities to children to grow and develop a personality of their own in the most accepted manner of society. Family bonding is the bedrock of the relationship between parents and children. Bonding can be strengthened through skills training on parent supportiveness of children, parent-child communication, and parental involvement.

- Parental monitoring and supervision are critical for drug abuse prevention. These skills can be enhanced with training on rule-setting; techniques for monitoring activities; praise for appropriate behaviour; and moderate, consistent discipline that enforces defined family rules.
- Drug education and information for parents or caregivers reinforces what children are learning about the harmful

effects of drugs and opens opportunities for family discussions about the abuse of legal and illegal substances.

- Brief, family-focused interventions for the general population can positively change specific parenting behaviour that can reduce later risks of drug.

Health

Health is the greatest wealth of a human being. Health is one of the basic human needs and access to health services is an undeniable right of everyone. In other words, health encompasses psycho-socio-somatic development of the human being so health services for reproductive and maternal and child health are the first line of action to reduce neglect and violence against children from their earliest moments of life. These services not only provide the possibility of preventing unwanted pregnancies and improving access to prenatal, post-natal and early childhood health care, but can also help strengthen early attachment and reduce the risk of parental violence against young children. In India many facilities are provided such as maternity services, home visitation programmes for new born baby by the health or community workers/volunteers. Therefore, the early identification of parents who need support can be achieved without any stigma. The routine checks on mothers and children are through maternity services, promoting safe pregnancy and childbirth, and through home visits by health workers. These give an opportunity to provide parent education, and to direct resources to 'high priority' families by identifying known risk factors and offering additional services.

Programmes focusing on family functioning, particularly on family management, problem-solving, and parenting practices, has existed for several decades. There is strong and consistent evidence showing them to be effective in reducing home and family violence against children, as well as other negative child health and development outcomes. The most successful programmes address both the internal dynamics of the family and the family's capacity for dealing with external demands. Caregiver education can also pre-empt the evolution of poor parent-child relationships, and provide a context in which to teach parents non-violent methods of discipline.

The earlier these programmes are delivered in the child's life and the longer their duration, the greater the benefits. Home visitation involves health professionals, social workers or trained volunteers in the assessment of infants and young children's needs and their parents' capacity to meet those needs, given the family's current social and economic situation. Personalized home visits aim to provide emotional support and training to promote positive parental knowledge, skills and behaviour, and to a certain extent to assess the family. Home visits also offer an opportunity to link a family with other community services as needed. The value of home visits by nurses health workers to the first two years of the child's life those who are living in socio-economic difficulty, the result will be found after 10 years because of social accountability or preventive force to reduce child abuse. The benefits to the visited families included a significant reduction in child abuse and neglect, as well as reductions in maternal alcohol/drug problems. Current evidence indicates that the most successful home visitation programmes focuses on families with an elevated risk of violence against the child, and begin in pregnancy and continue to at least the second year of the child's life, actively promote positive health behaviours, support the family in stress management, and address a range of issues that are important to the family. Programmes should be flexible in order to adjust to the changing needs of families. Parenting education, another successful and widely used prevention strategy, can be offered either in the context of home visitation programmes or independently. Programmers usually educate parents about child development and aim to improve their skills for behaviour management. Parents' and caregivers' positive behaviour management skills can be improved by developing an understanding of the importance of follow-through and consistency, rewarding and reinforcing positive behaviour, strategically ignoring minor negative behaviours, giving effective instructions, and implementing non-violent consequences for misbehaviour.

Parenting programmers should strive to strengthen the skills of both mothers and fathers. Parenting programmers are increasingly being implemented in middle – and low-income countries. Health workers are trained to provide parents with the knowledge and skills needed to meet the survival, growth, development and protection needs of their young children, and also to know when and where to go for specialised services. The initiative started in 2002; already it is clear that family doctors and nurses who attended the training programmes are more likely to engage in parent education. This initiative includes a specific focus on protecting children from all forms of violence, including physical punishment and other humiliating forms of discipline.

Many families need help in providing not only basic care but also stimulation and education for their children. Early Childhood Care and Development (ECCD) programmers are designed to achieve both of these objectives, and there is evidence that they can be effective in reducing the factors that engender violence in the home. In India through the Angnawadi worker a review of day-care programmers for pre-school children of economically disadvantaged parents found that the effects on the mothers' interaction with their children were positive, and that the mothers' gains in education or employment were beneficial for their families. Long-term benefits to children included improved behavioural development and school achievement, higher levels of employment, lower teenage pregnancy rates, higher socio-economic status, and decreased criminal behaviour.

Government should ensure that comprehensive systems to prevent violence and protect children are implemented at scale, in ways that respect the whole children and their family, their dignity and privacy, and the developmental needs of girls and boys. Further it should ensure that response systems should be co-ordinated, aimed at prevention and early intervention, linked to integrated services that extend across sectors – legal, education, justice, social, health, employment and other necessary services. Respect the views of the children in all matters and decisions which affect them should be assured. Governments have the obligation to develop evidence based standards to facilitate effective and sensitive service delivery for children in all corners of the society.

Education

The children have both a right to education and rights in education. Make sure that children receive an education a means of improving their status and make primary education compulsory, free and available to all. This means that institutions have to protect the right and interest of their students, and also to teach them how to respect the rights of any others. The rights based approach to education makes education the very foundation of the long-term campaign against violence of all kinds, including violence against children. Children raised in schools free of violence and taught to respect the rights of everyone to live in violence-free environments are the best hope for a violence-free future. The rights-based, child-centred approach requires that there is 'code of conduct' accepted by all members of the school community, establishing moral and social reference points and emphasising the values that underpin them, including the values inherent in the CRC and in other human rights conventions. Discipline should aim at positive reinforcement, constructive criticism, clear guidance and instruction. Except in extreme cases it should not promote measures that may impede a child's cognitive and emotional development.

Recent research on disciplinary regimes has made a distinction between positive line of action and reactive behaviour. Those that are positive line of action focus on prevention, and are generally based on careful research into what works, and they establish a legal framework, clear policies, clear rules of conduct and mechanisms for enforcement. The reactives are often based on ill treatment, abusive language and harsh punishments. That often involves suspending or expelling children, who only displaces the problem to another school, this line of action affects the community at a large. It should be avoided by school staff. Such type of on line action contravenes the fundamental rights of child that is enumerated in Article 21A *i.e.* 'Right to Education'.

The curriculum, teaching methods and the whole school climate should teach, illustrate and reinforce the principles of gender equality, human rights and non-violence and the skills to apply these principles in day-to-day life. They should also serve to increase children's resilience, so they could cope-up from violence and recover when it occurs.

School curriculum has been very 'content' and focused what to be taught, with less attention paid to learning skills and processes how it can be implemented, such as problem-solving, and decision-making, inquiry about a fact and moral values of life. It is necessary to teach children about the constructive human behaviour, so that they can protect themselves from harm, and take action to avoid harm to others in this rapidly changing regime. This kind of education is often called 'life skills-based education'. Life skills-based education should be part of a package that includes education on the principles of gender equality, human rights and non-violence and the principles evolved to put into practice.

This may involve dealing with highly personal and sensitive issues relating to the unique characteristics of each child, child's family background, religious and cultural traditions, and subjects once considered taboo were in discussion involving children. Dealing with such issues requires development not only of the curriculum but of appropriate teaching methods. This involves going beyond traditional route learning to encouraging children to ask questions, including their teachers, to relate their own experiences, and to express their own feelings and ideas as part of the learning process.

Social Policy

Society is the strong protective layer around the children and day by day that layer is diminishing due to nuclear families, urbanisation and loosing family value and it creates harmful environment for the children. A strong social policy is essential for supporting families and enabling them to thrive despite economic, social and psychological stress. At the society and community level support strategies are prepared and aim to raise awareness of child rights, and promote change in social and cultural norms, gender equity/equality, and non-discrimination. In every community there should be family support centres that can provide assistance in emergency situations and help to develop supportive networks providing quality child care facilities, pre-school, school programmers. Such programmers should target to include Government sector workers like police and magistrate and administrative staff, teachers, health workers, and the private sectors like parents, the educated/non-educated and common man. Further it is pin pointed to those families or children who need special care and protection. The other social policy like special protection for disable children; unemployment benefits; health insurance, income-generating programmes, food/nutritional supplementation for those who are in extreme needy family.

Government should improve the major areas; these are employment to adults, minimum wages, equitable land reform, equitable compensation in case of forced displacement, rural livelihoods like equitable access to facilities such as water supplies, roads and paths, transport systems, drainage, and sanitation. Women's income-generation programme which added more facility and reduces child abuse in family, because it creates equitable status in family and decision-making power to her.

Violence prevention among the children needs to be factored into 'macro-level' decision-making areas such as national poverty reduction strategies, policies to reduce social vulnerability, policies for local Government reform and administrative decentralization, the extension and improvement of services for health, education and community infrastructure and special care should be given for up-liftment of children's rights. The mechanisms, where by such policies are adapted and implemented at local level via community-based or group-based approaches require a close attention to do best in every respect.

Breaking the Silence

Silence is the best weapon in the hands of the children and they successfully use it. Due to this silent nature it is difficult to know to what extent adults are abuse children; abuse and neglect in all places and it may be inside the house or outside it may be common places like school, work place, or around the common place they reside. Many times it is found that abuse is very closely related to the victim child, abuser are abuse directly or indirectly ; however much they fear and dislike the violence they experience – do not feel they have any place to make their feelings known, or they may even consider that such feelings are 'legitimate'. Many feel shame or blame themselves, while others stay silent for fear of provoking further violence, or insensitive interventions which could make their overall situation worse. Within the general trend to lay more emphasis on child consultation as an integral component of programme planning and interventions with children, child-friendly methodologies for consultation and action-research have been developed. These, coupled with counselling and communications skills, have also been used to enable children to open up to adults they regard as safe about their intimate and painful experiences. In some small-scale examples, notably in India, children who have been trafficked by their families and have few trusting relationships with adults have organized themselves to provide mutual support and avoid further exposure.

Child help lines are gradually becoming more common: as already noted, discussion in confidence with a counsellor by phone allows some children to report what is happening to them and seek help. Help lines or hotlines have been set up by various NGOs in order to help children escape from abusive situations; they are used in many places of our country and it is found that children experiencing violence as domestic helpers in the homes of those who are not their parents or the poor parents who are addicted with alcohol or the care takers or in a stress situation.

When violence against children is suspected or disclosed, action must be taken to protect the children and often include mechanisms for reporting, referral, investigation and follow-up. Ideally, legal measures should be implemented in appropriate with health and social support approaches. Support and assistance without adequate protection can endanger the child's well-being and development; but a legal focus on investigation and protection with insufficient follow-up and parallel treatment can lead to severe and lasting damage both to the child and to the family. Research is urgently needed to identify effective support, help and treatment-oriented approaches to child protection and how they might be implemented in both high – and low resource settings. Although rooted in human rights and a clear framework of legislation, child protection systems operating at community level need to evolve in consultation with communities. While aiming for acceptance and trust, child protection workers must be made fully accountable within the context of the overall system and its accountabilities.

The potential for damage to the child increases with increasing frequency and severity of victimization over time. It is therefore important to identify violence as early as possible and intervene to stop it. Health professionals have an importance in child protection because, except in very remote rural areas, infants and small children are usually taken to the health centre on a routine basis. In countries with social service networks, they may also be seen occasionally or on a regular basis. Social workers in his or her duty get more occasions and contacts and provide an opportunity to detect violence against children that parents and caregivers may try to disguise as unintentional injury or illness. Given the pressure on health-clinic staff, they need training and capacity-building, as well as improved facilities. Since detection is not always straight forward, standardised guidelines and tools to assist professionals with assessments are essential. Training health workers to detect and manage violence against children appears particularly promising for pre-verbal infants who cannot describe what has happened and for all cases where detection depends upon observation rather than a first-person account. In many form of settings, the community based mechanisms are being established for monitoring violence in the home and the need for child protection. Most of these are in experimental stages, and structured evaluation is required before clear conclusions can be drawn. The Councils set up a database and monitoring system on children, including those who are at risk or who are victims of exploitation and violence; whose primary target is to reduce physical, emotional and sexual violence in the home and outside.

Economic Equality and Equal Opportunity

Today's world is facing two main and most critical challenges towards upliftment of the child, that are access to positive livelihood opportunities and the possibility of upward mobility by non-criminal means. There are some exemplary shows that policies that reduce the concentration of poverty in urban areas, *i.e* by improving employment, education, vocational training opportunities, may be effective in reducing violent behaviour by young people. If they have a personal stake in building a safe environment and that their aspirations are realisable within the law, the personal frustration and social tension that fuel violence may be considerably defused.

A framework of national political, economic and social policies therefore needs to be developed which prioritise growth, equity and sustainability in the harnessing of natural and human resources, and that replaces or rebuilds the deficits in social safety and security which have emerged.

The strong and consistent demonstration of a close relationship between high levels of economic inequality and increased homicide rates in adolescents and young adults indicates that policies which reduce economic inequality or minimize its effects may be of great value in preventing such violence. This appears to be especially relevant for males, since research indicates that the relationship between economic inequality and homicide is much stronger in males than in females.

Media Exposure and Its Impact

The media plays a vital role in guiding the society by reporting the child cases in every form, knowingly or unknowingly it exposes the trauma of the child. No doubt the social and moral responsibility of print and electronic media is to report the same to check the rampant practice/dare devil of the evil doors of the society.

Prevention of violence against children through the media will require co-operation at the individual and community levels, and the development of national strategies. Many contributors to the Study suggested the use of education campaigns for children and parents to inform them about the issues surrounding violence in and through the mass media, and particularly about Internet risks and safe Internet behaviour. Other strategies specifically aimed at the Internet include creation of 'watchdog' organizations which monitor offensive websites, and both regulation and self-regulation of the Internet industry. Better law enforcement measures are also called for, including criminal prosecution of people, who use the Internet to harm children, monitoring of known offenders once they have been prosecuted, programmes to prevent people becoming offenders, and treatment for offenders. Governments should ensure that initiatives to instil non-violent, non-sexist norms and values are carried out through media campaigns and strong leadership from public figures. Focuses should include eliminating sexual harassment and rape, and providing alternative models of masculinity, which do not support violence from men and boys.

Legal Provisions

Legal provisions are made on assault and criminal offence and which Constitutions prohibit *i.e.,* cruel, inhuman or degrading punishment; laws which prohibit cruelty, maltreatment or 'abuse' of children. But these laws are not specifically interpreted for prohibiting violence against children. Indian laws prohibit incest, rape and other sexual assaults; and also specify a minimum age of sexual consent or marriage, although this is often below the age of 18. Laws on criminal assault, as has been noted by the Committee on the Rights of the Child, are seldom interpreted as prohibiting physical chastisement, corporal punishment and all other forms of cruel or degrading punishment of children in the family and outside.

Between 1996 and 2006, the Committee on the Rights of the Child has recommended to countries that they take steps to prohibit all corporal punishment. In 2006, the Committee adopted a General Comment – a statement of its authoritative interpretation of the CRC – on the right of the child to protection from corporal punishment and other degrading forms of punishment. The Committee emphasises that the first purpose of law reform to prohibit all corporal punishment within the family is preventive: "to prevent violence against children by changing attitudes and practice, underlining children's right to equal protection and providing an unambiguous foundation for child protection and for the promotion of positive, non-violent and participatory forms of child-rearing".

The Committee also emphasises that the principle of equal protection of children and adults from assault, including within the family, does not mean that all cases of corporal punishment of children by their parents that come to light should lead to prosecution of parents: "The *de minimis* principle – that the law does not concern itself with trivial matters – ensures that minor assaults between adults only come to court in very exceptional circumstances; the same will be true of minor assaults on children. States need to develop effective reporting and referral mechanisms. While all reports of violence against children should be appropriately investigated and their protection from significant harm assured, the aim should be to stop parents using violent or other cruel or degrading punishments through supportive and educational, not punitive, interventions".

India has introduced measures to criminalise abuse by intimate partners; measures which broaden the definition of rape have been introduced, thus dispelling the notion that violence among intimates is a private matter, thereby helping to shift social norms. However, legal changes do not guarantee social change, where it is not backed up by public and professional education. Laws passed to reflect CRC obligations which are not linked to widespread public education and which clash with cultural norms and accepted practices may be systematically ignored. Combating harmful traditional practices such as FGM, for example, cannot be achieved by legal change alone, even though legal systems should and must condemn them.

Legal changes must be accompanied by education programmes directed at officials, parents and children. In some cases, legislation exists but is insufficient; imprecise or insensitive implementation of it can compound children's victimization rather than relieve it. Some existing legislation is so inadequate that it penalises child victims instead of family perpetrators; in these circumstances, it may actually reinforce the possibility of violence against children.

To protect dignity of a young child many social and court orders passed against the child right when a young girl below the age of consent or marital union has been raped and become pregnant, marriage to the rapist can be imposed upon her. Legislation and laws against so-called 'honour killings' may impose more lenient sentences than on other homicides, or perpetrators may be exonerated by traditional justice systems; and children sold into prostitution may bear the brunt of social disapproval or be treated as criminals. Preventing violence against children in the home and family setting requires legal reform to reach beyond laws which are directly concerned with violence.

Factors such as alcohol availability, family planning services, pre – and post-natal care, social security, mental health, substance abuse treatment, birth, death and marriage registration, and levels of environmental toxins are just a few examples of important factors that are sensitive to legal and policy reform.

Children Participation

Participation of children at all level is an essential object. Where the abuse occurs, children without proper understanding or they may think that no one believes them or due to fear they keep silence and they suffer silently. In such circumstances, special efforts are required to make it possible for them to feel safe to discuss violent incidents. Systems of local Government can play an important role in this regard; whether in the context of centralisation/decentralisation/ privatisation system, they need to include the views of children and young people.

Youth empowerment was fundamental to developing neighbourhood strategies for violence prevention. Creating associations or support groups for specific groups such as children living in the street or survivors of child abuse, with the objective of developing a common identity and solidarity around their own issues, can be an empowering experience. It can be the springboard for taking action on behalf of their own agenda, including the promotion of other child rights, and for undertaking joint activity on behalf of vulnerable peers suffering from domestic abuse, risk of child marriage, discrimination or school exclusion.

Participation is thus a key principle to be applied in all efforts to prevent and eliminate violence to and by children; as well as educating children and parents. Governments should work with the industry to devise global standards for child protection, undertake research on protective hardware and software solutions, and funds education campaigns on safe use of the new technologies. Governments should also pursue law enforcement approaches, including criminalizing those who make, distribute, possess or profit from pornography involving children.

Involving children in developing and implementing programmes is important in building personal knowledge, attitudes and skills, ensuring programmed relevance and ownership, and ultimately in improving programme outcomes found that teaching environments that put children at the centre of the learning experience, so that teachers listen to their concerns and needs, are more likely to address violence effectively. Where children participate in discussing and addressing violence, discussion is more open and more likely to result in specific strategies. All regions have identified benefits, some unexpected, of involving children in the development and implementation of programmes to address violence in schools. Children can provide a comprehensive snapshot of their experience of violence in their schools, thus giving staff information they need to take action. Involving children serves as effective intervention in it, in that matter it helps to heal children through the disclosure of experiences and sharing of feelings and it teaches the staff about children's experiences and feelings, and this in turn changes staff attitudes and behaviours.

General Recommendations

(i) *Policy and Legislation:* The present National Policy on Children needs revision and there is a clear and established need for a separate National Child Protection Policy. In addition, every State should set up a State Commission for the Protection of Rights of the Child and formulate Plans of Action for Child Protection at the district and state levels for better implementation.

There is also a clear and established need for a National Legislation to deal with child abuse. The proposed legislation should address all forms of sexual abuse including commercial sexual exploitation, child pornography and grooming for sexual purpose. It should also deal with physical abuse including corporal punishment and bullying, economic exploitation of children, trafficking of children and the sale and transfer of children. The legislation should also look at mechanisms of reporting and persons responsible for reporting. This must be seen in the context of the fact that more than 70 per cent of the child respondents do not report the matter of sexual abuse to anyone. It has also very clearly emerged that the largest percentage of abusers are persons within the family or persons in position of trust and authority.

The legislation should address such issues also, and mere enactment of law is not the solution and it requires from every corner support of society and people to become truthful.

(ii) *Protocols:* In order to enhance the standards of care and build a protective environment for children in the country, there is a need to develop standard protocols on child protection mechanisms at the district, block and village levels, defining roles and responsibilities of each individual and agency. Such protocols should also lay down standards and procedures for effective child protection service delivery including preventive, statutory, care and rehabilitation services for children. An effective community-based monitoring mechanism needs to be put in place to ensure accountability at various levels. Monitoring should be based on indicators of performance such as quality of services and levels of child friendliness.

(iii) *Scheme on Child Protection:* So far child protection has been dealt within a piecemeal and dilatory way with allocation of minimum resources reaching out to a miniscule numbers of children in difficult circumstances. The results of the study point to the need for a national scheme. Such a scheme should identify vulnerable families and children, prevent vulnerabilities and provide services to those in need. The scheme should strengthen statutory support services provided under the Juvenile Justice (Care and Protection of Children) Act 2000 for children in need of care and protection and children in conflict with law. With the allocation of adequate financial and human resources, the scheme should help create a protective environment for children through strong service delivery mechanisms, outreach services and effective interventions.

(iv) *Outreach and Support Services:* The study has revealed that the majority of abuse cases take place within the family environment, the perpetrators being close family relatives. A child who has been abused or continues to be in an abusive situation, needs a variety of services, including professional help in the form of trauma counseling, medical treatment, police intervention and legal support. Such a system should be established under the scheme on child protection. Further, the existing Child line service providing emergency outreach services to children in difficult circumstances should be expanded.

Migration and rapid urbanisation have forced a very large number of children onto the streets. Such children survive by begging, working, scavenging, rag picking, etc. It is essential to provide outreach services to these children through bridge education, night shelters and vocational skills, so as to get them off the streets, reduce their vulnerability and enable them to sustain themselves in the society.

(v) *Tracking of Missing Children:* Children go missing for a number of different reasons. Difficult and abuse situations at home often force children to run away; economic compulsions make them move to urban and semi-urban areas in search of a living; and sometimes they are trafficked for domestic work, other forms of labour or commercial sexual exploitation. Annually, large numbers of children go missing and there is little attempt to track them or trace them. Such children are most vulnerable to all forms of abuse and exploitation. Not only should they be tracked but existing mechanisms for their rescue, rehabilitation, repatriation and reintegration should be reviewed and strengthened while keeping in view the best interests of the child.

(vi) *Sharing Responsibility:* Child protection is a shared responsibility, and for any intervention to be effective, there should be a synergy between efforts being made by different stakeholders to address the issues. There is a need to create a mechanism that will make such a synergy possible. These may include child protection mechanisms at village, block, district and state levels that involve parents, elected representatives of urban and rural local bodies, teachers, *anganwadi* workers, medical practitioners, police and social workers and responsible members of public among others.

(vii) *Capacity Building:* All the above recommendations regarding formulation of a new policy, legislation, scheme and strengthening of the service delivery mechanism, assume the creation of a cadre of trained personnel, sensitized to child rights and protection of children. In order to create this cadre, in the first instance, schools of social work and universities should offer specialised courses on child rights, protection and counselling. Further, child rights and protection issues should be integrated into the curricula of administrative institutes, police training academies, law colleges, medical colleges, teacher training schools, etc., so that the professionals passing out of these institutions have both the sensitivity and the knowledge to deal with these issues. Capacity enhancement and skill up-gradation of those, who are already working in this sector, are also essential. Further, there is a need to regularly up-grade the skills and capabilities of the civil society organizations.

Parents and caregivers are primarily responsible and accountable for the safety and security of the children in their care. The results of the study suggest that somewhere parents have not lived up to these expectations. Therefore, there is a need to enhance parenting skills, knowledge of the subject and sensitivity, which will help them to handle situations of child sexual abuse. Life skill education of children to enhance their knowledge and capacity to deal with abuse is essential. It is proposed that this should become an integral part of the school curriculum.

(viii) *Gender Equity:* Equity is possible if social norms ensure that the girl child lives in a non-abusive environment in which she is cared for and respected. Discrimination of girls results in their lower enrolment in schools, higher levels of malnutrition, trafficking of girls for sexual exploitation, child marriage and their non-participation in decision-making in the family etc. These imbalances were needed to be addressed by bringing about attitudinal changes in people regarding the value of the girl child.

Empowerment of adolescent girls should be done by making them aware of their rights, orientating them on the subject of abuse, instilling life skills including knowledge of child-birth and child rearing practices, HIV and AIDS and personal hygiene among others. The adolescent girl component of ICDS should be strengthened.

Government, NGOs and civil society should make efforts to instil non-sexist norms and values through advocacy and communication strategies and campaigns using electronic, print and folk media and through open discourses on gender equity with involvement of public figures. Focus should be on elimination of discrimination and abuse of girls and on creating awareness of existing legislations.

(xi) *Awareness Programmes:* The media should be used to spread awareness on child rights. Debates and discussions with participation of children can be a regular feature on electronic media in order to enhance people's knowledge and sensitivity on child protection issues. While media coverage of child protection issues is desirable, it is essential that the coverage is done in such a way that it prescribes to high ethical standards of reporting such as avoiding disclosure of the identity of the child victim to reduce the child's trauma and prevent re-victimization of the child. It is also essential to obtain informed consent of the child in cases of reporting. All these measures will protect the child from the stigma attached to abuse and prevent sensationalisation of the issue. The Ministry of Information and Broadcasting and media self-regulatory authorities should take necessary action to develop ethical standards for the print and electronic media and to implement them.

(x) *Documentary Findings:* The national study has thrown open various avenues of research which need to be undertaken in order to further strengthen some of the findings emanating from the study. These areas for research could include:

- Child Rights.
- Violence and its impact on children.
- Causes and impact of different forms of child abuse.
- Issues around children in conflict with the law.
- Corporal punishment in schools.
- Urban poverty and children; working children with special reference to child domestic workers and children working in small scale projects, *dhabas* and tea stall's etc., among others.
- Neglect of children.
- Gender discrimination.
- Orphans and the adoption system.
- Good practices in protection should be documented and shared to facilitate qualitative improvement at all levels.

11. *Child Protection and Service Management:* The biggest challenges in child protection are the creation of a database of all child protection services, linking of lateral services, creation of a knowledge base, and tracking of missing children, all of which have to be addressed at the grassroots level. The database, therefore, should be developed at the district level itself with upward and lateral linkages.
12. *Participation of Child:* Children's voices need to be heard by everyone. All forums addressing issues of child rights should have adequate children's representation with the opportunity for them to express their views. For example, school curricula should be developed with the active participation of children; children should be involved in development of the district child protection plan, children should be involved in management of schools and institutions, etc.

Apart from the general recommendations, there are certain specific recommendations regarding different evidence groups that emerged which are given below:

Children in School

The study has indicated beyond doubt that schools as compared to other situations are the safest place for children and therefore efforts should be made to increase the enrolment and retention of children in school by adopting innovative, child friendly methods of teaching. Adequate infrastructure including sanitation facilities, keeping in the mind the special needs of the girl child, will encourage enrolment and retention of girl children in schools.

The high incidence of corporal punishment in schools is a clear indicator of the absence of use of positive disciplining techniques by teachers. Some State Governments have banned corporal punishment in schools. However, corporal punishment continues unchecked. There is a need for formulating a central legislation banning corporal punishment and creating a system where in such cases are not only reported but strict action taken against abusive teachers and principals and if it is managed by the committee the managing authority is to be penalised in accordance to law.

Children's participation in meetings held by village education committees on issues dealing with school functioning, governance and maintenance of facilities at school should be encouraged at every sphere.

Children at Work

There should be better coordination at National, State, District and Block/Ward/Village levels for the following:

Rescuing children from banned occupations and their repatriation and mainstreaming into appropriate education streams. Poverty alleviation schemes specifically targeting families of working children, repatriated working children and children at-risk of falling into child labour.

In the NCLP districts, children should be empowered by inclusion of knowledge on child protection issues and life-skills within the NCLP curriculum. State level guidelines and protocols should be formulated for the rescue, repatriation and rehabilitation of child domestic workers.

Children in Institutions

India continues to use institutionalization as a method of providing services to children in difficult circumstances. Although internationally it is now an established fact that institutionalization is not in the best interest of the child, yet, in countries like India, where the number of children in need of care and protection is very high and the non-institutional methods of care are not developed, the institutionalization of children will continue till alternatives are identified. In the light of this the following observations are made:

1. A child in need of care and protection is one who has not been given proper care by his parents. Observation homes are intended for temporary reception of children during the pending of any inquiry regarding them under children Act. That should provide the children not only with accommodation, maintenance and facilities for medical examination and treatment but also with facilities for useful occupations. When the family atmosphere is not conducive special homes may be provided to rectify them in each district and each block and village level which should be manned by sensitive and trained personnel.
2. In existing institutions, standards of care should be established and maintained. Institutions under the Juvenile Justice (Care and Protection of Children) Act, 2000 are corrective institutions. Children in conflict with the law in these institutions should be provided with all the opportunities to reform and develop into responsible citizens. But one thing must be adhered too that is children in observation home should be kept occupied and the occupation should be congenial and intended to bring about to adopt adaptability in life aided at bringing about self-confidence and picking of human virtues. The present state of the existing institutions leaves a lot to be desired.
3. The caretakers and often caregivers of the institutions are also abusers. This behaviour of the caregivers destroys the faith and trust of the child and completely alienates

him/her from society itself. This should be prevented by strict monitoring and supervisions of homes, maintenance of detailed records of children, deinstitutionalization of children, wherever possible, and training and sensitization of caregivers in institutions.

4. Every home should have a management committee whose members, along with members of the community and civil society, should be involved in the efficient running of these institutions and prevention of abuse. Children should also be encouraged to participate in the management of the institutions. All children have the right to live in safety and dignity in a protective and nurturing environment, both at home and in the community. This is possible by creating awareness of their rights, especially their right to protection, in parents and other stakeholders, putting in place laws to punish those who abuse and exploit children and taking appropriate action to strengthen accountability on the part of government and non-government agencies and the civil society.

For the first time, in India, an effort has been made to understand the extent and magnitude of different dimensions of abuse of children in the country with the hope that the findings will pave the way towards a better understanding of the factors leading to abuse of children and measures to prevent them, thus creating a such a caring and nurturing environment. There is an urgent need of observation homes where children are kept in some purposeful activities like watering the plants, help in cooking and cleaning the institutions so as to keep their body and mind in a fit condition. The home emphasises more on their educational and vocational training, in this home juveniles are provided with food, clothing, shelter and medical psychiatric services including and guidance is the need of hour.

Child Abuse Treatment

Victims of childhood abuse seek therapy for a number of reasons, but rarely just because of the history of abuse. Many survivors minimize the effects of the abuse. Therapists see clients for eating disorders, depression, anxiety disorders, substance abuse disorders and more who have histories of abuse. It is important to help the client deal with the abuse as well as the psychological problems they report. Counselling in the form of individual and possibly group therapy can take two years or longer. The goal of undoing life-long damage can be very difficult because the damage pervades every aspect of the client, and because there may be physiological changes to the client that can't just be 'counselled' away. Medication can be useful for the symptoms of depression, anxiety and other symptoms, but should never be dispensed in the absence of counselling for the root of the problem. Later the survivor may need to undergo couples or relationship counselling when he or she heals to the point of finding a long-term relationship. For children, play therapy and family therapy can be helpful. Treatment of the after-effects of abuse must be tailored to the needs of the specific individual, but usually involves a variety of long-term considerations that may include legal concerns, geographical relocation, and housing or employment as well as immediate medical or psychiatric care.

Medical and Mental Abnormality

In addition to requiring immediate treatment for physical injuries, abused children and adults often need long-term psychotherapy in order to recover from specific mental disorders and to learn new ways of dealing with distorted thoughts and feelings. This approach to therapy is known as cognitive restructuring. Specific mental disorders that have been linked to childhood abuse include major depression, bulimia nervosa, social phobia, Munchausen syndrome by proxy, generalised anxiety disorder, post-traumatic stress disorder, borderline personality disorder, dissociative amnesia, and dissociative identity disorder. Abused adults may develop post-traumatic stress disorder, major depression, or substance abuse disorders. At present, researchers are focusing on genetic factors as a partial explanation of the fact that some people appear to react more intensely than others to being abused.

Legal Considerations

States need to be even more vigilant for the protection of the children. It is general obligation of the State but legal consideration is different in its context; every person shall be presumed to be innocent unless he is proved guilty by competent court of law. In this liberalised market the child became a 'commodity' being the ultimate object; child's body has been commoditized, commercialized and marketed as a product. Now-a-day's child across the country are being sexually abused and exploited. When it happened inside the home and school etc., it is called abuse. When it happened out side and payment involved it is called prostitution. Truly, both the issues are concerned with child protection. Law alone is not just sufficient to curb and control such a cancerous evil operating in the society, which has very deep roots. The concern for protection of children through realisation of certain rights accepted by all nations, all the state parties, appreciate the urgency of such uniform rights and commit to uphold than by creating as enabling condition within the respective countries contextual realities around the children of specific community and of specific society are often referred to as a hurdle to come to terms with C.R.C. This allusion is a plea to cover up the failure to protect the children by the caregiver. CRC is not only relied of guidance but also a measuring yard stick. CRC is a comprehensible and indivisible package. Its partial application may hurt children rather than benefit them. Need of survival and right to survival are not situated at opposite ends of the same spectrum. They are not inseparable. Those opposite ends can be linked with child centred social policy. But without proper implementation of socio-economic programme of the Government, the abolition of child labour is not possible unless financial security to poor is ensured. This process must begin with challenging unhealthy and damaging myths and stereotypes regarding perpetrators and survivors of child sexual abuse. But the medical jurisprudence has no exception about the legal consideration. The professionals as such Medical professionals and, increasingly, religious professionals as well, are required by law to report child abuse to law enforcement officials, usually a child protection agency. Physicians are granted immunity from lawsuits for making such reports. Adults in abusive situations may encounter a variety of responses from law enforcement or the criminal justice system. In general, cases of spouse abuse, stalking, and sexual abuse by professionals are taken more seriously than they were two or three decades ago. Many communities now require police officers to arrest the aggressor in domestic violence situations, and a growing number of small towns as well as cities have shelter house for family members. Who are the victims of domestic violence. All major medical, educational, and legal professional societies, as well as mainstream religious bodies, have adopted strict codes of ethics, and have procedures in place for reporting cases of abuse by their members. Abuse in the workplace, however, is still a relatively new area of concern, and people affected by it have relatively few legal protections or resources available to them. It is imperative and urgent to prevent them from bearing cancerous children face, exploitation and suffering in the society, mental and physical both, millions of children live under especially difficult circumstances, as orphans, street children, destitute children, abandoned children, working children, etc. It is found that a large number of children under the age group of three to five die every year due to diarrhoea and several millions suffer from other dangerous diseases such as; Polio, Hepatitis, and AIDS, etc. Therefore proper health, education and environment for the children are the imperative needs of the Hour. As a plant that needs protection, nourishment and proper environment to grow into a big form bearing tree, child also needs protection, promotion, nourishment, and proper environment to grow into a useful and responsible citizen to serve the future nation.

6 Conclusions and Suggestions

Concluding remarks is an essential element of any debate or discussion, analysis or exploration for brevity and certainty. The scope and subject matter of the present thesis is, no doubt, a study of utmost importance in quantitative terms. The worthiness of the study depends on the qualitative presentation of conclusions. Besides, the researcher endeavours to offer important suggestions to plug loopholes in the existing child abuse laws. The purpose is not fault-finding, but to make the legislations as well as the various organizations to effectively work and meet the needs of the society.

Of the creation of God, the indivisible and Almighty, child is considered to be most intellectual gene. Man in greed for socio-economic progress and in his curiosity to probe into and understand the philosophy of the creation of God, man has initiated, the exploitation of not only his co-human and other beings, but also the beauty of natural resources. In this process man has reached an extreme stage of exploitation to his own generation and ecology in every respect. This could be endangering to the very existence of human being and natural living of all beings. Today's personality theorists see children as the complex products of both heredity and environment. They are no longer merely massive clay ready to be shaped by a capricious environment. It is therefore our duty, to protect these tender flowers from dangerous affect of excess exposure and heat. Child abuse is an ulcer which exists in the society from time immemorial. The concept of abuse to child is a different aspect and difficult to define but the researcher turned out every method to describe it elaborately in a proper manner within this confined work. All abuses against children and child right violations have no remedy in the paradigm of law. The most notable one is that in this research the judicial activism of Supreme Court in the defined areas, is by and large, not only defensible but also indispensable, in this present context of affairs taking into consideration, the judiciary can continue to command an overwhelming confidence of the people only when it can expedite the process of administration of justice.

Child abuse is a multidimensional problem that requires a multidisciplinary, multiagency team approach for successful intervention to arrive the destination. Of course, 'imagination lit every lamp' no doubt man has developed an ample of resources or measures to meet the emerging problems and research on 'child abuse' is one among them. Child abuse, especially when it happens within the context of a relationship of power and trust, is the most fundamental violation of childhood. As such 50 per cent abuses are persons known to the child or in a position of trust and responsibility. However, abhorrent it may seem, the reality is that child abuse exists. And the tragedy is that it is most often perpetrated upon innocent and vulnerable children by adults, who are ideally supposed to uphold the rights of children, and work in their best interest. All children were vulnerable to abuse behind closed doors of homes across our country. Children are being tortured, beaten and killed. It is happening in rural areas, towns, cities and in metropolitans as well. It is crossing all social classes, genders, racial lines and age groups. It is becoming a legacy being passed on from one generation to another. There is a lot of variations in the form of its occurrence in urban and rural areas and in upper/middle class and lower class families in the society. History always shapes the future and provides a function of the present; it opens a limelight path for the future.

The research in this core subject is demanding a strong will power to find out the unknown happenings of various abuses. Child sexual abuse has to be handled carefully, as it is a very delicate matter. Most of the cases are going unnoticed because of ignorance. Child sexual abuse affects individuals greatly both physically and mentally. The affected children grow into problematic children and they are unable to face the problems. The condition of tortured victims who survive is still worse. To make the child abuse movement successful, a holistic approach is needed and comprehensive step should be taken by preventing and controlling crime against children, otherwise a major threat will prevail with society, family and victim.

The concepts of Globalisation, Liberalisation and Modernisation and Cyberism have given rise to many more challenges in the legal arena to find out the problems. But the problems like child exploitation, neglect, abuse, child trafficking, cyber crimes, pornography, sex tourism, terrorism and other modern organized crime problems are peculiar and enormous in nature. It is very difficult to sort out and solve them in accordance to law with in a stipulated period of time but this is not an impossible task. It is a fact that child abuse illuminates and influences the entire legal system of any civilized society.

The systematic study of material evidence and sources are necessary to establish the fact and to reach new conclusions. Mere enactment of laws in a bulky way relating to negligence, exploitation and abuse are not the remedy. In this context the Supreme Court not only declares the law but also makes the law by liberal judicial interpretation.

There is also a lack of comprehensive legal and policy measures on child abuse in India. In this regard concerted efforts should be made to influence law to offer protection to all children against violence and abuse. It is also a point that

State Government alone cannot eliminate the gigantic child abuse problem but the social ethos can be changed gradually within the means.

It is a fact that number of rape cases of pre-matured girls has been rising since last few years. A survey of teens and +2 college students found that rape accounted for 67 per cent of sexual assaults in girls. Apart from sexual abuse and rape, pushing, slapping, punching, stalking and emotional abuse are other forms of domestic violence against children. However, child domestic workers are even more vulnerable for their social and economical powerlessness. There can be multiple effects of abuse on children like self-devaluation, dependency, mistrust, and re-victimization, withdrawal from the people, emotional trauma, deviant behaviour and interpersonal problems. The vulnerability factors and prevalence of different forms of abuse are few factors that this research attempts to bring to the foreground. These factors, prevalence and other dynamics have been discussed in detail in the previous few chapters. Every kind of attention has thrown up information on the extent and magnitude of child abuse and girl child neglects. While the situation is an alarming, it is an important to take cognizance of the fact that the study was not done with the intention of creating fear and alarm. In this context, child abuse has to be properly understood in order to prevent and protect the social environment paving the way of peace and morality.

Child sex tourism has now become an International crime. In order to tackle this problem effectively an extra territorial laws should be made so that sexual offenders not only the foreigners but also those who are on the host land and engage themselves into sex with children, can be prosecuted and punished. Various crimes generally occur in the society and these are; rape, sodomy, exposure to pornographic material, fondling, forcible kissing and sexual advances, among others. Community centres can do much help to control most of these crimes. Therefore to educate the parents for guiding properly to be aware of these situations and to have the skills are necessary for good parenting. Recognition and awareness are an essential elements for an effective prevention. Parents and children should be made aware of such abuses and carefully heed to what their children want to share without fear and favour. There is nothing wrong in seeking help tips for prevention of abuses. Successful family support activities and child abuse prevention programmes are designed to promote these protective factors, which are enumerated below:

- Parental confidence and knowledge.
- Strong bonds between parents and children.
- Family social connections – to decrease isolation.
- Family knowledge of child development.
- Effective problem-solving and communication skills.
- Concrete support in times of need.
- Children are socially and emotionally capable.
- Healthy marriage.

It is crystal clear that child abuse is prohibited significantly by law. There were societal patterns of abuse of children especially runaway children, especially in the developed cities who were at high risk for sexually transmitted diseases and HIV. They often worked 18 to 20 hours a day, frequently in hazardous conditions and suffered sexual and mental abuse. Discrimination against children with HIV/AIDS is a problem. The Government has been taking various pro-active measures to tackle this stigma. However, considering the magnitude and extent of the problem, essentially though it is a socio-economic problem, it requires concerted efforts from all sections of the society to solve the problem. In India, legislative initiatives for the promotion and protection of children's rights are sparse and the enforcement impoverished.

There were enormous numbers of children needing care and protection, while on the other hand there were not enough schemes or sufficient budgetary allocations to deal with them. As sexual abuse is more sensitive issue, it is necessary that everybody should understand the acts which create a criminal offence. Prevention of child abuse and neglect is still an uncharted field in many parts of India and similar situation as prevalent in the State of Orissa also. In a State like Orissa which has 47 per cent of its population below under BPL (Below Poverty Line), children are the most affected ones and their concerns mostly remain sidelined in the State's priorities. The vulnerability of children in Orissa is manifested in myriad forms. Droughts, floods, epidemics, acute food shortage, female foeticide and chronic hunger leading to starvation deaths are quite common. Incidences of violence, abuse, neglect, maltreatment against the children are still rampant in the State. Children living in poverty are deprived of their rights to survival, health and nutrition, education, participation and protection from harm, exploitation and discrimination. The issues of protection, abuse, neglect and discrimination of children become all the more compounded in a predominantly rural, traditional and patriarchal society doubly burdened with gendered and caste biases with poverty being a cross cutting feature. All these factors influence the lives of children in the State of Orissa. Often it is believed that it is a big problem and the only solutions to child abuse lies within the legal system. In many places, there is little recognition of child abuse among the public or health professionals. But especially the higher judiciary has an onerous responsibility to safeguard the Constitutional mandate through golden interpretations. Social justice, Human rights and the rights of the child are three threads of the same texture. That social justice must begin with child but the State is the organ manifesting social changes. Human rights protection is protected by the Welfare State. The Welfare State is a social myth widespread in modern capitalistic society. Human rights and social organizations should take up the issues of sexuality and minorities as a part of their mandate for social change. Education development for the welfare of the society is an essential tool to uplift the downtrodden class of the society. Education is also a key agent of change capable of breaking the cycle of violence, not just against children but among adults too. It can encourage children to learn self-respect, respect for others and how to express their feelings and negotiate for what they want without resort to physical or psychological violence. There is estimation by child welfare organization that about 500,000 street children nationwide lives in an abject poverty. Ignorance is also another factor to indulge them to win the bread and butter for their living. Society, like a family, must provide the basic needs of children, as a first priority for its own survival and development. Investment in children is the priority investment for the future of society.

Demeaning children is a grave threat to the society. It was also observed that to carry the issue of child protection forward there was a need to create an enabling environment, through a legislation to address such issues of child abuse, make a policy on child protection, formulate interventions and outreach services and create an information base on child protection. This study would be a small step in that direction. This research work consists of collection of data from various sources in this direction. It is felt that projection made in this endeavour would be of some use for the policy-makers as well as for the policy implementers in their long-term and short-range planning efforts.

After a deep and thorough analysis of various child abuse factors and the prevailing legislative framework in the country, the researcher feels it necessary to offer the following suggestions to make-policy changes to eliminate the menace of child abuse.

Suggestions

- Parents should participate voluntarily in the campaigns against child abuse and should suggest protection strategy to their children in child-friendly manner.
- Schools should be encouraged to institutionalize 'Personal Safety Education', a curriculum for children that aims at prevention of sexual abuse by helping children participate in their own protection through age-appropriate information, skills and self-esteem.

- School teachers have to be trained to handle the misbehaving students through guidance and counselling instead of corporal punishments.
- Community based educational programming that addresses the stigma of rape and sexual abuse are imperative in order to encourage victims to come forward and receive help and the emotional support they need from their families and communities. Communities must be made aware of options of recourse and how to address the issue with sensitivity.
- Investment is necessary in social, housing and educational programmes that strengthen families and improve linkages and social networks within and between different income groups. Governments should analyse the impact of public policies on communities and their children. Local Governments in particular should be encouraged to take steps for prevention and make violence prevention explicit in urban rehabilitation schemes and rural development programmes. Governments, and their national and international partners, should strive to integrate efforts on violence against children as a key element of sustainable and culturally sensitive poverty reduction programmes.
- Programming for support of orphans and street children are important to protect them from exploitation. Children need protection, vocational training and empowerment in order to avoid abuse. Community centres and safe houses could help with this dimension. Also, these highly vulnerable children need to have a trustworthy, effective outlet in order to report abuse and receive the help they need to cope with the trauma.
- There is a need to create a mechanism which may include child care and protection mechanisms at village, block, district and State levels which involve parents, elected representatives of urban and rural local bodies, teachers, *anganawadi* workers, medical practitioners, police and social workers and responsible members of public among others.

- There is a necessity to conduct awareness raising campaigns and education programmes through strengthened formal and non-formal education on *rights issues* to change attitude at home and break the cycle of inter-generational violence.
- Parents must be informed about the ill effects of child labour and they should be motivated for education of their children and they should also be informed that the poor income of their children would not improve the economic conditions of their families.
- There is dire need of providing social support system to the families and children engaged in labour, which is almost non-existent.
- It is imperative to take immediate and effective measures to secure the prohibition and elimination of the worst forms of child labour as a matter of urgency.
- Provisions are necessary for the rehabilitation and social reintegration of children removed from the worst forms of child labour by ensuring access to free basic education and whenever possible provide appropriate, vocational training.
- Promotion Inter-State cooperation to assist in addressing child labour and its root causes, inter alia, through social and economic policies aimed at poverty eradication, granting funds while stressing that labour standards should not be used for protectionist trade purposes.
- Mainstream action relating to child labour into national poverty eradication and development efforts, especially in policies and programmes in the areas of health, education, employment and social protection is the need of hour.
- Government should take appropriate measures to enhance the economic conditions of the needy and poor families, so that they can provide education to their children.

- Professionals at the frontline who are working with children, such as teachers, medical professionals, school counsellors, police personnel should be sensitized and trained to appropriately respond to child sexual abuse, for prevention, detection and management perspectives.
- Steps should be taken to Review of existing laws against child sexual abuse for boys and girls (with focus on family) at a regional level, including customary laws and systems for implementation.
- Strengthening and building capacity of parents' associations, mother and father groups, on parenting techniques and work with older sisters, brothers, and friends for child protection at family level are necessary. Work with men and boys on prevention of child sexual abuse and gender-based discrimination is also essential.
- To strengthen and to build capacity of children's task forces/groups against child sexual abuse including awareness raising, prevention and action, using peer-to-peer techniques and child-friendly methods are considered very useful.
- Regular qualitative and quantitative data collection of child sexual abuse in family and other settings for advocacy and strategizing mechanisms for protection and prevention of child sexual abuse.
- NGOs and other civil societies should be made aware of sexual abuse of children, They should be trained to respond to this issue and they should be helped to address it as a crosscutting concern within their existing framework of activities with children and adult stakeholders. The Department of Social Welfare will have to initiate steps as soon as possible to establish a special cell to deal with the physical, emotional and sexual abuse of children and create awareness among the public on these vicious social issues.
- It is necessary to conduct sustained campaigns in society at large to promote social norms that emphasise respect and non-violence and gender equity. Governments

should ensure that initiatives to instil non-violent, non-sexist norms and values are carried out through media campaigns and strong leadership from public figures. Focuses should include eliminating sexual harassment and rape, providing alternative models of masculinity which do not support violence from men and boys.

- It is highly necessary to implement policies and programmes to discourage the system of dowry and establish community support system for the protection of married girls.
- There is a need to Increase awareness of boys and girls about sexuality and provide psychosocial support through rehabilitation homes for girls subject to sexual violence and other kinds of violence.
- Initiative should be taken to conduct legal audit in selected areas *e.g.*, inheritance, divorce, marriage to identify and address male bias through a participatory and educative process, involving the community and policy-makers.
- Necessary steps should be taken establish programmes to break the culture of silence through help lines and involvement of neighbours and relatives and establish community based councils to deal with home based violence, balancing responsibility in addressing gender based violence between state and family.
- It is an essential to stop the use of mass media and information technologies, including the Internet and electronic games, in violence against and sexual exploitation of children. As well as educating children and parents, Governments should work with the industry to devise global standards for child protection, undertake research on protective hardware and software solutions, and fund worldwide education campaigns on safe use of the new technologies. Governments should also pursue law enforcement approaches, including criminalising those who make, distribute, possess or profit from pornography involving children.

- The media should be used to spread awareness on child rights. Debates and discussions with participation of children can be a regular feature on electronic media in order to enhance people's knowledge and sensitivity on child protection issues.
- Stringent Laws should be enacted to completely curb child abuse and sex tourism in the country, which will prevent the child trafficking indisputably. There is a plethora of children's issues that the state needs to tackle aggressively *i.e.*, begging, child labour and sex work being the most urgent ones.
- In the absence of any cogent remedy against cyber offences, where children are the innocent worst victims, it is high time that children should be given proper advanced technology education to control misuse and enable children not to become innocent victims of cyber crimes.
- The legal practitioners forum should voluntarily advocate at free of cost in the child abuse cases for the benefit of the children and in parallel way for the benefit of the growth of country.
- It is very important to prioritise attention to gender issues and their links with violence. Governments must acknowledge the pervasive impact of entrenched gender stereotypes on the nature of violence in and around schools. Male students, staff and community members, must be actively encouraged as strategic partners and allies; and along with female students, staff and community members, must be provided with opportunities to increase their understanding of how to stop gender discrimination and its violent manifestations.
- There is a need to provide effective reporting systems for children. Governments should ensure that effective reporting systems for children are established. They should allow the children who are victimised to reach trained professionals, who can, if necessary, refer the case

to social workers, or health professionals, or law enforcement agencies. In community settings, these may include child help lines as well as formal mechanisms such as community advocates for children.

- It is considered as very important to implement civil registration universally, including the registration of births, deaths, and marriages. Governments must ensure free and accessible civil registration free certification, and must remove penalties for late registration. The process must be advocated widely and facilitated and implemented in cooperation with local Government, hospitals, professional and traditional birth attendants, police, religious and community leaders, and other partners in order to ensure universal uptake.
- It is none the less important in the present situation to conduct further research on identifying the further causes of home-based violence and promote responsible and gender sensitive reporting by the media.
- It is to be borne in mind that a conscious and conscience approach to prevent child abuse in all forms is the need of hour, which enlightened citizenry must take into cognizance.

Bibliography

Agarwal, S. C., "Computer Ethics, Child Sexual Abuse, Pornography and the Regulation of Child Pornography on the Internet", *CBI Bulletin,* Vol. 10, January 2002, pp. 7-11.

Anuradha, K. and V. Uma, "Listening to Children – Affirmation of their Right to Participation", *JAJS,* Vol. 3, No. 2, pp. 37-50.

Baruah, Arunima, *Child Abuse,* Reference Press, New Delhi, 2003.

Biggeri, Mario and M. Ratna, "Child Labour in Industrial Outworker Households in India", *Economic and Political Weekly,* Vol. 44, No. 12, 2009, pp. 47-56.

Borra, Neera, *"Exploitation of Children in Jaipur Gem Industry II Health Hazards of Gem Polishing",* *Economic and Political Weekly,* Vol. 23, 2001, pp. 131-138.

Chakraborty, Sudeep, "Universal Child Rights in the Disclosure on Child Labour", *Social Action,* Vol. 58, No. 4, 2008, pp. 381-92.

Chauhan, B. B. S., Child Abuse: An Organized Crime", *Indian Police Journal,* Vol. 47, 2000, pp. 66-72.

Daligand, Liliane, "Child Abuse: The Victimology Aspect", *CBI Bulletin*, Vol. 26, February 1992, pp. 38-42.

Devi, Rameshwari and Ravi Prakash, *Social Work Practice*, Mangal Deep Publications, Jaipur, 2001, p. 42.

Forehand, C. Straurs and K. K. Smith, "Characteristics of Children with Extreme Scores on the Children's Depression Inventory", *Journal of Clinical Psychology*, Vol. 13, 1994, pp. 227-231.

Ganguly, Thukral, Enakshi, *Status of Children in India Inc.*, HAQ: Centre for Child Rights, New Delhi, 2005.

Geetha, C. V. and H. Venkatalakshmi, "Parents and Teachers Attitude towards the Education of the Visually Impaired Children in Special and Integrated Schools", *Journal of Community Guidance and Research*, March 2009, p. 16-17.

Gerain, Swapan, "Prevention and Management of Child Abuse", *Indian Journal of Social Work*, Vol. 56, July 1995, pp. 31-48.

Gupta, Srinivash, *Child Abuse: Growing Menace, Lex et Juris*, Vol. 5, Nov., 1990, pp. 34-36.

Hegde, K. S., *The Directive Principles of State Policy: The Constitution of India*, Discovery Publishing House, New Delhi, 1986, p. 72.

Hughes, J. N., "Cognitive Behaviour Therapy with Children in Schools", New York: Pergamon Press, 1988, pp. 267-78.

Joshi, Harish, Leela Visaria, Rajesh Bhat, "Children Without Childhood", Ahmedabad Study Action Group, Ahmedabad, 2006.

Kacker, L., S. Varadan and P. Kumar, Study on Child Abuse: India 2007 [monograph on the internet]. New Delhi: Ministry of Women and Child Development, Government of India, 2007.

Kannappan, R., "Intervention as an Adjunct to Drug Therapy for Childhood Depression", *Journal of Community Guidance and Research*, Vol. 26, No. 1, 2009, pp. 3-10.

Kapoor, H. L., "Horrible Increase in Child Abuse", *PRP Journal of Human Rights,* Vol. 6, Oct-Dec., 2002, pp. 5-7.

Kaul, S. K., J. "Access to Justice", *Nyaya Deep,* New Delhi, Vol. VII, No. 4, Oct., 2006, p. 12.

Kazi, Ashraf U. and Farisa Tasneem, "Existence of Child Labour in the 21st Century and Human Rights: International Perspectives and Legal Implications", *Bangalore Law Journal,* Vol. II, No. 1, June, 2007, pp. 1-24.

Koolwal, Mahesh, "Illegitimate Child vis-à-vis Human Rights", *Journal of Human Rights,* Vol. 38, 2008, p. 207-213.

Kumar, Krishna, "Rural Children – Fighting the Educational Bias" *Times of India,* 1st February 1995.

Kumari, S. Kusuma, "Abolition of Child Labour: Chasing a Mirage of Reality", *Supreme Court Journal,* Vol. 25, June 2007, pp. 40-48.

Kydd, John W., "Preventing Child Maltreatment: An Integrated Multi-sectoral Approach", *Health and Human Rights: An International Journal,* Vol. 6, No. 2, pp. 34-63.

Manoharan, Arlene, "A Critique of the Juvenile Justice Act 2000 in the Context of the Adoption Issue", Voluntary Health Association of India, New Delhi, 2002, p. 4.

McDonald, R. and E. N. Jouriles, "Marital aggression and Child Behaviour Problems: Research Findings, Mechanism, and Intervention Strategies", *The Behaviour Therapist,* Vol. 14, pp. 189-92.

Mehera, Jyothi, "Impact of HIV/AIDS on Children in Manipur: Rapid Assessment Study", Manipur State AIDS Control Society, 2001. pp. 79-84.

Mehra, Jyoti, "Reducing Risk Behaviour Related to HIV/AIDS and Drug Abuse Among Street Children", National Report, Ministry of Welfare, UNDCP, WHO and NACO, 1996, p. 39.

Mishra, Lakshmi Dhar, *Child Labour in India,* Oxford University Press, New Delhi, 2000.

Mohanty, Bimalendu, "Orissa: Yesterday, Today and Tomorrow", Nur Publishers, Bhubaneswar, 2003, p. 16.

Mukherjee, Dharjati, "Change of Societal Attitude Imperative", *Yojana,* November, 2006, p. 50.

Mukhopadhyay, Arun, "Child Welfare and Distributive Justice", *Social Welfare,* November 1998, pp. 17-18.

Narain, Arvind, Child Sexual Abuse; Issues Relating to Disclosure and Best Interest of the Child, Lawyers Collective Vol. 15, April. 2000. pp. 7-15.

Nath, G. B. and Ratnapriya Mishra, *"Linking Trade with Labour Standard", The Issue of Child Labour in India,* Discovery Publishing House, New Delhi, 1998, p. 67.

Nayar, Anil, "Enough Funds, but no Attention", *The Hindustan Times* (Delhi Edn), dated 1st May 1995.

Pagare, Deepti, *et al.,* "Sexual Abuse of Street Children Brought to an Observation Home", Maulana Azad Medical College, Department of Community Medicine, New Delhi, 2004, p. 6.

Panda, Saumya, "Health and Violence: A Perspective", *Bharatiya Samajik Chintan,* Vol. III, No. 1, April 2004, p. 13.

Pandey, P. N. and C. P. Mishra, *Child Labour in Glass Industry,* A. P. H., New Delhi, 1996.

Paranjape, N. V., *Criminology and Administration of Criminal Justice,* Central Law Agency, Allahabad, 1979, pp. 69-70.

Pasricha, Ravinder Kaur, "Violation of Child Rights and Victimization of Child Labourers: Working in Restaurants and Dhabas", *Indian Journal of Criminology and Criminalistics,* Sept-Dec., 2007, pp. 56-63.

Patel, Mamta, 'Abused Children in Print Media', *Indian Police Journal.* Vol. III, No. 3, July-Sept. 2006, p. 69-70.

Patil, V. Shivraj, "Sexual Abuse and Children", *Delhi Judicial Academy Journal,* Issue 1, Vol. 4, Mar, 2005, pp. 18-22.

Patnaik, Raghunath, "Vulnerability of Children through Cyber Crimes", *Indian Bar Review,* Vol. XXX, No. 2 and 3, 2003, p. 405.409.

Paul, Valsamma, "Sexual Abuse of Children – Need for Legislation", *Indian Bar Review,* Vol. 32, (1 and 2), 2005, p. 114.

Pradeep, Bhargava, Kanchan Mathur and Shobhita Rajagopal, 'Understanding Childhood Poverty in Rajasthan', Childhood Poverty Research and Policy Centre (CHIP) Report No. 16, London, 2005.

Prakash, S. B. N., "Criminal Justice System and Juvenile or Child in Conflict with Law", *Karnataka Law Journal,* Vol. 15, 2009, pp. 9-24.

Qureshi, Mohd. Ishaque, "Child Exploitation: Violation of Human Rights", *Aligarh Law Journal,* Vol. XIII, 1998, p. 34.

Radhakrishna, "Childhood Dreams in the Dums", *The Tribune,* 28th January 1993, p. 4.

Raizada, Ajit, "Reflections on Sexual Exploitation and Abuse of Children in India", *Madhya Pradesh Journal of Social Science,* Vol. 5, No. 2, 2000, pp. 1-21.

Rani, N. Usha, "Welfare of Women and Child", *Andhra Law Times,* Vol. 5, 2008, pp. 35-36.

Rao, S. Venugopal, "Law Relation to Children", *Indian Journal of Public Administration,* Vol. 15, 1990, pp. 157.

Reddy, C. Sheela, "Dimensions of Juvenile Crime: An Indian Perspective", *South Asia Politics,* Vol. 7, No. 3, August 2008, pp. 29-35.

Rehm, L. P., "A Self-control Model of Depression, Behaviour Therapy", *Journal Community and Guidance and Research,* New Delhi, Vol. 8, 1977, pp. 787-804.

Rekha, Wazir, "Newly Emerging Needs of Children: Towards Widening the Policy Agenda in South Asia", *Indian Journal of Human Development,* Vol. 2, No. 1, January-June 2008, pp. 13-44.

Rout, Bhikari Charan, "Justice of Juveniles: An Analysis", *Crimes,* Vol. 1, Part-II, February 2002, p. 355.

Rufus, D., "Child Abuse: An Overview", *Indian Police Journal,* Vol. 56, Jan-March, 2009, pp. 28-37.

Saith, Ashwani and Rekha Wazir, "Children of India: Rights and Opportunities", UNICEF Working Paper Series, 2010, p. 17.

Sarawat, Rita, "Child Labour", *Yojana*, p. 49.

Sarkar, Dibyajyoti, "Child Labour in India: An Introspection", *Labour Law Journal*, Vol. 2, May 2008, pp. 1-11.

Sarma, A. M., *Aspects of Child Welfare and Social Security*, Himalaya Publishing House, Bombay, 1985. p. 56.

Scott, J., "Cognitive Therapy for Depression", *German Journal of Psychiatry*, Vol. 1, 1998, pp. 15-30.

Sehgal, Uma A., "Child Abuse in India: A Theoretical Overview", *Indian Journal of Social Work*, Vol. 52, July 1991, pp. 293-302.

Sekar, Helen, *Child Labour Legislation in India – A Study in Retrospect and Prospect*, V. V. Giri National Labour Institute, New Delhi, 1997, p. 71.

Sekhar, Shashank, "Child and the Law: A Globalised Perspective", *Karnataka Law Journal*, Vol. 1, No. 5, March 2008, pp. 11-16.

Sen, Sankar, "Trafficking in Women and Children", *Journal of the National Human Rights Commission*, Vol. 3, 2004, p. 43-56.

Sengupta, Arjun, K. P. Kannan and G. Raveendran, 'India's Common People: Who Are They, How Many Are They and How Do They Live?', *Economic and Political Weekly*, Vol. 43, No. 11, 15 March 2008, pp. 49-63.

Sharma, B. K., 'Sexual Abuse of Children', *The Indian Police Journal*, Jan Mar., New Delhi, 2004, pp. 81-87.

Shashank, "Child and the Law: A Globalised Perspective", *Karnataka Law Journal*, Vol. I, No. 5, March 2008, pp. 11-16.

Siddique, Ahmad, *Criminology: Problem and Perspectives*, 4th Edition, Eastern Book Company, 1997, p. 264.

Sikri, A. K., J. "Human Rights and Indian Judiciary", *Nyaya Deep*, New Delhi, Vol. VII, No. 4, 2006, p. 57.

Singh, Kamaljeet and Harish Verma, "Growing Child Sex Tourism in Third World Countries: An Overview", *Civil and Military Law Journal*, Vol. 43, No. 3-4, July-December, 2007, pp. 114-118.

Singh, Subhash, "Growing Problem of Child Abuse and Neglect", *Criminal Law Journal*, Vol. 100, September 1994, pp. 81-88.

Singh, Surender J., "Citizen of Future Era" The Tribune, April 22, 1990. p. 7.

Souda, Naveen, "Child Labour in India", *Andhra Law Times*, October 2007, pp. 21-23.

Srinivas, K. L. and Pravesh Kumar Varadan, Report of the Ministry of Women and Child Development, Government of India, Supported by Save The Children and UNICEF, 2002.

Srinivasan, K. and Chander Shekhar, "Reviewing Reproductive and Child Health Programmes in India", *Economic and Political Weekly*, Vol. 42, July 2007, p. 27-28.

Srivastava, S. C., "Child Labour: Law, Policy and Its Enforcement", Kashmir University Law Review, Vol. 14, No. 4, 2007, pp. 1-26.

Surekha, Raman, "Violation of Innocence: Child Sexual Abuse and the Law", *The Lawyers Collective* Vol. 10, No. 11, October-November, 1995, pp. 4-7.

Swami, Ranganathananda, *Children Humanity's Greater Assets*, Bhartiya Vidya Bhawan, Bombay, 2nd edn, 1995, pp. 7-10.

Tiwary, Ashok, "Child Care: Socio-Legal Measures", *Indian Journal of Criminology and Criminalistics*, Vol. 28 (1), Jan-April, 2007, pp. 11-19.

Tripathy, S. N., *Child Labour in India – Issues and Policy Options*, Discovering Publishing House, New Delhi, 1996, p. 9.

UNICEF, The State of the World's Children 2006 – Excluded and Invisible, New York, 2005.

Vibhute, K. I., "Reforms in the Law Relating to the Child Sexual Abuse in India", *Cochin University Law Review*, Vol. 2, No. 29, Jun 2005, pp. 99-184.

Vijay, Vasanty, "Justice to Destitute Children", *Social Welfare*, Vol. 38, No. 8, November 1991, pp. 13-14.

Virani, Pinki, *Bitter Chocolate – Child Sexual Abuse in India*, Penguin Books India, 2000.

Wani, Afzal, M., "Abolition of Child Labour: International and National Perspectives", *Nyaya Kiran*, April-June, 2007, pp. 29-43.

Reports

Annual Report, 1999-2000, Department of Women and Child Development, Ministry of Human Resource Development.

Annual Report, CACL, 2001.

Annual Report, NCRB, 2009.

Award Digest, *Journal of Labour Legislation*, National Labour Institute, New Delhi, 2002.

Census of India, 2001, Series 22, Orissa Paper - 1 of 2001.

Centre for the Prevention and Healing of Child Sexual Abuse, "Prevalence and Dynamics of Child Sexual Abuse among School going Children in Chennai", Chennai, 2006.

Education for All – Early Childhood Care and Education, NIEPA, GOI, 2000.

National Initiative for Child Protection – A Resource Book published by CIIF, NISD, Ministry of Social Justice and Empowerment with support of UNICEF, 2000.

Report on National Seminar on Implementation of Child Labour Projects, National Resource Centre on Child Labour, V. V. Giri National Labour Institute, New Delhi, 1997.

Statistics on Children in India (Hand Book), (1989-99), National Institute of Public Co-operation and Child Development, Government of India.

Study on Child Abuse, 2007, Ministry of Women and Child Development, Government of India.

Study Report on Sexual Abuse of Children in India, National Commission for Women, 2001, p. 67.

The Bureau of Police Research and Development, "Child Abuse: An Overview", BPRD, New Delhi, 2009.

Websites

wcd.nic.in/childprot/jjact2000.pdf

wcd.nic.in/NAPAug16A.pdf

wcd.nic.in/nationalcharter2003.htm

www.equalityhumanrights.com/human-rights.

www.fiuindia.gov.in/downloads/PMLA2002.pdf

www.un.org/Depts/dhl/resguide/spechr.htm.

www.un.org/disabilities/convention/conventionfull.shtml

www.unicef.org/crc

www.unicef.org/india/Child_Marriage_handbook.pd

www.un.org/documents/ecosoc/cn6/1995/ecn61995-5add1.htm

Child Trends, Available at http://www.childtrends.org

Newspapers

The Dharitri, March 15, 2002.

The Indian Express, March 13, 2006.

The Indian Express, May 15, 1997.

The Indian Express, September 19, 2004.

The Indian Penal Code, 1860, Section 354/375/376/377.

The New Indian Express, July 23, 2007, p. 3.

The New Zealand Law Journal 1977 No. 4, p. 66

The Samaj, Bhubaneswar, May 11, 2011, p. 2.

The Samaja, August 21, 2001.

The State of the World's Children, Unicef Report, 2000, p. 13.

The Times of India, April 12, 2002.

The Times of India, April 14, 2007, p. 4.

The Times of India, April 14, 2007, p. 4.

The Times of India, New Delhi, August 13, 2009, p. 3.

Index